IMAGES
of America

LOST ANN ARBOR

VIEW FROM DR. FRIEZE'S BALCONY, 1885. This view from Dr. Frieze's balcony at the southeast corner of Cornwell and Ingalls, looking northeast, shows the Wall Street Bridge in the background. Frieze, a former acting president of the University of Michigan, built his home here to enjoy the lovely view of the Huron River valley.

IMAGES
of America

LOST ANN ARBOR

Susan Cee Wineberg

ARCADIA
PUBLISHING

THE U-M CAMPUS IN 1864. This engraving of the University of Michigan was based on a painting by J.F. Cropsey from the 1864 *Washtenaw County Plat Map*. Shown are the Medical College, Chemical Laboratory, Law Department, Mason Hall, and South College.

CONTENTS

ACKNOWLEDGMENTS

This was a sad and wrenching book to write because Ann Arbor has lost so many fabulous buildings. Yet it is by no means comprehensive. Many of the images of "lost" buildings have been used by Grace Shackman in previous books in the Arcadia Images of America series, and my attempt here has been to avoid using previously published photos and to use unpublished images whenever possible. The format of this series has allowed me to present selected subjects of our lost architectural past with an attempt to address those subjects as comprehensively as possible. However, this book should not be mistaken for a complete examination of all of Ann Arbor's lost architecture.

I would like to thank my friend Grace Shackman and her husband Stan for all the help and support they have given me. Others who have provided photos and moral support are Wystan Stevens, Louisa Pieper, Ray Detter, Penny Schreiber of the *Ann Arbor Observer*, Judy Chrisman, Sue Kosky, Carol Horn, Rob Godspeed, Lisa Dengiz, and Robert Samborski. Ari Ingimundarson, Harold Borkin, and Adrienne Kaplan helped us with computer problems. The staff of the Ann Arbor District Library, especially Dietmar Wagner, were very helpful. Wystan Stevens helped tremendously by editing copy at short notice. I owe a tremendous thanks to the staff of the U-M Bentley Historical Library and to Karen Jania in particular, who always went above and beyond the call to help. But I owe my greatest thanks to my husband Lars Bjorn who has been my rock throughout the past year of work and who has worked tirelessly on behalf of the project.

INTRODUCTION

Ann Arbor might have developed like most of the small towns in southern Michigan had it not been for one major event in its history. Thirteen years after its founding by John Allen and Elisha Rumsey in 1824, it was designated the site for the state university of Michigan. This event, which occurred in 1837 only months after Michigan became a state, served to determine the nature and growth of the town. Today, with the University as its major employer, Ann Arbor consistently enjoys the lowest unemployment rates in the state and has produced an artistic, intellectual, and progressive environment unusual for its relatively small size of 110,000. But dynamism has a price. The city has lost much of its architectural heritage and lacks the concentration of some major architectural styles found in some Michigan cities.

Another factor in the 20th century affecting the demolition of significant buildings was the automobile. The car had a huge impact on American life, and changed patterns of housing, transportation, and work. As the state highway system grew, once elegant residential streets became major thoroughfares. This inspired a migration to other neighborhoods with less traffic. First, the old mansions were converted to restaurants, funeral homes, clubhouses for church groups, or gas stations. Some grand homes, such as those on East Huron, were demolished for car-related purposes—for gas stations, parking lots, used car lots, or new car showrooms. While in many towns, large residences would have remained as rooming houses or funeral homes, the prosperity of Ann Arbor allowed them to be purchased and demolished. Elegant mansions encircling the university were demolished for university expansion.

With growth of the university came growth in the town, and a demand for expanded government services. Only a handful of municipal buildings survive from the 19th century, and these are mostly schools. We still have the 1886 Fire Station (now the Hands-On Museum), but other older public buildings—city hall, courthouse, and library—have all been replaced with newer buildings. Continuous growth required larger facilities and many buildings were removed because they were no longer adequate to meet community demands.

Ann Arbor was mainly settled by "Yankees"—most from upstate New York, but also from Connecticut, New Hampshire, and Massachusetts. After 1825 they arrived by way of the recently opened Erie Canal. The canal allowed easy travel between Albany on the Hudson River and Buffalo on Lake Erie. Then a boat ride took travelers to Detroit, and from there the "wild" west (i.e., the Michigan Territory) opened up. The lower tier of counties between Detroit and Lake Michigan is full of towns settled in the 1820s and 1830s, many with names inspired by the successful Greek Revolution against the Turks (1821–1832).

When planning first began for the university, the University Regents were optimistic and hired New York architect Alexander Jackson Davis to design a campus. Three years later when work began, they had no money to pay for the elaborate Gothic Revival design proposed. So, simple buildings of stucco-over-brick, scored to look like masonry and decorated at the roofline with the Greek "key" or meander patterns, were built by masons from New England. Their decidedly conservative tone and classical appearance reflect the New England influence. The original campus had four professors' houses and one classroom building that also served as a dormitory. Originally called the Main Building, it was renamed Mason Hall in honor of the late Stevens T. Mason, the "boy governor" of Michigan. This building survived, with many additions, until 1950. Of the four professors' houses, only one remains, as the U-M President's House.

Following the adoption of a state constitution in 1850 which gave the university constitutional status and greater independence, the Regents were required to hire a president. The first, Henry Philip Tappan, was an "Eastern" man well-traveled in Europe and determined to bring the

German model of higher education to the Midwest to create "an American University deserving of the name." Tappan knew the conservative East would oppose his plans, and felt Michigan offered him a golden opportunity. Tappan quickly built many buildings, but his personality and ideals collided with powerful interests in the state and he was fired in 1863.

Changes in architectural taste became faster with dissemination of books and the ease of acquiring materials after the arrival of the railroad in 1838. After the mid-19th century, magazines promoted architectural styles and from-plan books published in that era, especially those of Andrew Jackson Downing. Buildings of the 19th-century campus reflected the current thinking of the time, just as they do now. What is reviled in one era is hailed in another. Some of us now mourn the loss of towered Romanesque behemoths of the late 19th century which were universally disliked in the early 20th century. The University's unique status under the Michigan Constitution allows it to decide which buildings remain and which will go. This has, of course, sparked protest from time to time.

Germans came to Ann Arbor from Wurttemberg in Swabia, especially after the failed revolution of 1848. They brought their own building traditions, and commercial blocks with arched windows and corbelled brick designs reflect this. Many of these buildings survive, a testimony to the conservative bent of the German population, and also to brick construction and better fire protection. Of course, other forces of "progress" were at work, encouraging the replacement of wooden buildings by brick ones, and "old-fashioned" structures by modern ones. Fire also played a key role in destroying architectural landmarks, as did the willful destruction of some beloved structures despite public outcry.

Celebration of the city's sesquicentennial in 1974 and the American bicentennial in 1976, sparked a renewed interest in historic preservation and spurred the creation of several historic districts in Ann Arbor. The Old West Side Historic District, established in 1978, was the first of many neighborhoods across the country to see their working class heritage as a key element of local identity and community spirit. Comprising some 900 buildings, many without architectural distinction, the Old West Side Historic District was a pioneer in protecting a total environment and not just outstanding individual buildings. The district recognized the importance of context and continuity. It was the first such district in Ann Arbor to be placed on the National Register of Historic Places.

Other neighborhood districts followed, including the Old Fourth Ward district, established in 1983, and the Washtenaw-Hill districts in 1980 and 1986. In the commercial parts of town, remaining Italianate commercial blocks on Main Street are protected by the Main Street Historic District, as are the early 20th-century buildings on South State Street. Historic designation doesn't prohibit demolition, but it does require approval by a commission appointed by the mayor and city council. Despite outcries from some quarters over the regulatory nature of these districts, most Ann Arborites agree they have been good for the city. Alumni returning for class reunions can still recognize the town of their youth. And citizens continue to enjoy pedestrian-friendly streetscapes created by old buildings.

One

Town Life Revolves around the Courthouse

Two days after Allen and Rumsey registered their plat in Detroit in 1824, territorial governor Lewis Cass's commission explored making Ann Arbor the seat of Washtenaw County. They cleverly recommended that it be on private property. Allen dutifully donated an entire block for a courthouse at the northeast corner of Main and Huron. Three successive courthouses have stood on this site and it continues today as the seat of county government. Every city has at least one historic building whose loss is universally mourned, and the second courthouse is at the top of Ann Arbor's list. Though its legal functions are now carried out in modern buildings, nothing has replaced it as a symbol of the heart of downtown. Businesses quickly went up around Courthouse Square, and Huron and Main became the literal center of town, as "ground zero" in the numbering system, dividing the town into north, south, east, and west. The county's first courthouse was an unassuming brick structure built in 1834. It played a pivotal role in the "Frostbitten Convention" of 1836, after which Michigan became a state. It was replaced in 1878 by a Renaissance Revival confection designed by G.W. Bunting, with statues of justice, a clock tower, and a bell. Set in a greensward, it was the central gathering place for political rallies, speeches, and community events. It inspired poems by Robert Frost. It was glorious!

The building slowly deteriorated in the 20th century. The clock tower was removed and parking lots were carved out of the lawn. Finally in 1955, a new structure was built around it, after which it was demolished for parking. A similar fate befell nearby buildings that formerly housed lawyers, doctors, dentists, banks, hotels, and an opera house.

ANN ARBOR'S SECOND COURTHOUSE, 1916. Courthouses on central squares were architectural focal points for county seats throughout the U.S. They were gathering spots for political rallies, facilities for registering deeds, and they provided courtrooms for the county. The 1878 courthouse was designed by G.W. Bunting and stood at the center of town, dispensing justice for more than 75 years. Ambrose Pack, a Spanish-American War veteran and later postmaster and sheriff, posed for the memorial to the dead of the Civil and Spanish-American wars. The memorial was moved to Forest Hill Cemetery in 1954, when construction began for a new building. When the new courthouse was finished, records were passed through the windows of the old building to the new building, and then the old was torn down. The site of the old building now serves as the parking lot for the new one.

ANN ARBOR'S FIRST COURTHOUSE, 1864. John Bryan built the first courthouse in 1834 on land donated by John Allen. Court was held on the second floor and the rooms on the first floor were lawyers' offices. The register of deeds and the county clerk were in two smaller buildings flanking it. Local historian Cornelia Corselius noted in 1909 that tanners were permitted to cure the hides on the courthouse fence, the bloody side uppermost and being "most offensive to both sight and smell." In December 1836, this building was the scene of the "Frostbitten Convention," at which Michigan's statehood was approved after delegates agreed to relinquish claims to Toledo to Ohio, and accept the Upper Peninsula instead.

EAST SIDE OF MAIN STREET BETWEEN HURON AND LIBERTY, 1880S. The courthouse tower looms over Main Street in this lively stereo card. Streets were unpaved and dust was a fact of life. The building just in front of the tower was demolished in the early 1920s for the First National Building, but remarkably, most of this block remains, though most of these old landmarks have lost their cornices.

TOWNSPEOPLE GATHER TO HEAR U-M PRESIDENT TAPPAN ANNOUNCE THE BEGINNING OF THE CIVIL WAR, 1861. U-M President Henry Philip Tappan reads a telegram on April 15, 1861 to tell of the firing on Fort Sumter and the outbreak of the Civil War. People gathered on the courthouse lawn, not the campus, for this was a community affair, and men were encouraged to organize military companies. Businesses on Huron Street can be seen in the background.

12

WILLIAM JENNINGS BRYAN, C. 1900. In one of his three failed bids for the Presidency, renowned orator Bryan (under the umbrella) spoke before a rapt audience on the courthouse steps. He later became famous during the 1925 Scopes Trial, when he opposed Clarence Darrow and argued against the teaching of evolution.

A BLIMP CIRCLES THE COURTHOUSE TOWER C. 1935. In 1917, local officials voted to set the clock tower on Eastern Standard Time, stating the tower was built by popular subscription and was being lighted by the city, and thus should be controlled by the city. The local newspaper noted that the clock had been a $1,000 gift from businessman Luther James and that he'd be turning in his grave over that little lie.

13

THE TOWERLESS COURTHOUSE, 1952. The removal of the tower was one assault of many against the courthouse. It was perceived to be a fire hazard and removed in 1948, but as one newspaper writer noted, the two statues of the Roman goddess Justitia were now attracting more attention (the other two had disappeared long before.) Alas, the statues no longer held their scales of justice and seemed to be waving at passersby.

THE COURTHOUSE LAWN BECOMES A PARKING LOT, 1951. Another insult to the courthouse was the use of the lawn for parking. By the 1950s, the courthouse was considered overcrowded, unsafe, and inefficient. Papers were stored under stairwells and mice and rats were a problem. Note the sign for the Preketes Sugar Bowl Café (on right) and the sizable increase in traffic. Soon the Civil War Monument would be moved to Forest Hill Cemetery.

14

THE NEW COURTHOUSE IS BUILT AROUND THE OLD, 1954. Construction of the new courthouse, designed by Ypsilanti architect Ralph Gerganoff, was well under way in February of 1954. The tall building across the street still stands today at Main and Huron, as does the other bank building, today covered in black granite. Michigan's Calhoun County was also getting a new courthouse built around its old one.

THE GREGORY HOUSE (MASONIC) AT THE NORTHWEST CORNER OF HURON AND MAIN, 1890s. Hotels and business blocks encircled the courthouse, with doctors' and lawyers' offices, masonic organizations, banks, and bookstores. The Gregory was the epitome of Italianate architecture in 1862 but by the 1960s it had become an eyesore. It was "modernized" in 1964 with a checkered skin of blue and white panels but was destroyed by fire in 1969, and the vacant lot served as a People's Park for over a decade. An adjacent building came down in 1985 and One North Main now occupies the entire site.

15

FRANKLIN HOUSE, NORTHWEST CORNER OF HURON AND MAIN, 1856. The Gregory House replaced the Franklin House, an 1837 brick hotel that housed several members of the faculty for the recently opened university. An invitation from February of 1859 for a "supper and cotillion party" had "carriages in readiness at six o'clock." Music was provided by the Winegar & Minnis Band.

COOK'S HOTEL, SOUTHWEST CORNER OF HURON AND FOURTH AVENUE, 1871. The "new" Cook's Hotel of 1871 replaced the 1830s Cook's Hotel, across from the courthouse. Always a "temperance house" (no alcohol), Cook's had five incarnations, the last in 1911 as the Allenel, so named to honor Ann Arbor founder John Allen. It was demolished in 1964 for a Sheraton Hotel that is now the Courthouse Square Apartments.

THANKSGIVING MENU, COOK'S HOTEL, 1883. Thanksgiving at Cook's Hotel was celebrated with gusto and game and a veritable groaning board of foods to choose from. A surprising item here is California salmon, indicating the effect trains had on the transporting of foodstuffs packed in ice. French terminology reveals the high-class tone set by this hotel.

MENU.

SELECT OYSTERS
SOUPS
MOCK TURTLE, aux quenelles
CONSOMME OF CHICKEN
FISH
CALIFORNIA SALMON, oyster sauce
Hollandaise Potatoes
REMOVES
YOUNG TURKEY—cranberry sauce
SADDLE OF MUTTON—currant jelly
DOMESTIC GOOSE—apple sauce
SIRLOIN OF BEEF—with mushrooms
GAME
HAUNCH OF VENISON—currant jelly
Horseradish   Queen Olives   Celery
ENTREES
RABBIT PIE, Hunter style
PEACHES with RICE, a la Conde
CREME FRITTERS, a la Reine
MACARONI, au gratin
Shrimp Salad   Cabbage Salad
VEGETABLES
Boiled Potatoes   Sweet Potatoes
    Mashed Potatoes   Cold Slaw
        Green Corn   Tomatoes
PASTRY AND DESSERT
Thanksgiving Pudding boiled, brandy sauce
Apple Pie   Mince Pie   Pumpkin Pie
Sponge Cake Macaroons Cocoanut Cake
Vanilla Ice Cream   Assorted Nuts
Apples   Catawba Grapes   Cider
    Coffee   Tea

17

OLD POST OFFICE (BEAL BLOCK), 200 NORTH MAIN STREET (NORTHEAST CORNER OF MAIN AND ANN), C. 1892. One of the grandest buildings in town was the Beal Block, constructed in 1882 by publisher Rice Beal and designed by Ann Arbor architect William Marshall. A glorious example of Richardsonian Romanesque, it had a unique feature—a layer of moss for soundproofing between the outer and inner walls. It served as the post office from 1882 to 1909 and was a gathering place for townspeople who had to pick up their own mail until home delivery began in 1886. Professor Emil Lorch, head of the U-M School of Architecture, requested the unusual arched doorway for the grounds of the architecture school (now Lorch Hall) when it was demolished in August of 1935. Junius Beal, later a U-M Regent, poses by his bicycle and Dr. William F. Breakey (U-M Professor of Dermatology) is sitting in the carriage. The building was demolished in 1935 and the lot remained empty until the first Kroger supermarket was built at the site. This later became the Red Shield Store of the Salvation Army. Today it is the site of the Washtenaw County Annex housing the Public Records Office.

AERIAL VIEW OF ANN STREET FROM COURTHOUSE, C. 1917. A view from the courthouse looking northwest shows buildings on Ann Street and beyond in 1917. It also shows the short-lived home of *The Ann Arbor Times News* at 105 East Ann, designed in 1916 as the first structure built solely for newspaper publication. It was demolished in 1940 and replaced by a Kroger supermarket. That too was demolished in 1989. Today it is the site of the Washtenaw County Annex Building.

EAST ANN STREET LOOKING NORTHWEST, C. 1900. Detroit photographer J.H. Cave caught the scene on Ann Street in 1900 looking towards Main Street. The buildings in the center survived, but those on either side have not. On the far left is the Beal Block, and on the far right is the Maynard Block, demolished c. 1960 after harness maker J. Frank Malloy finally closed up shop.

19

POST OFFICE, NORTHWEST CORNER OF ANN AND FOURTH, 1929. This Greek Revival structure was built in 1840 and served as the post office until 1853. For its last 15 years it was Magioncalda's Confectionery, hence all the advertisements. It shared the street with the Raftopoulos Billiard Parlor and the Hing Lee Laundry, as well as Malloy Harness. It was demolished in 1929 and replaced by a gas station, now the Bellanina Day Spa.

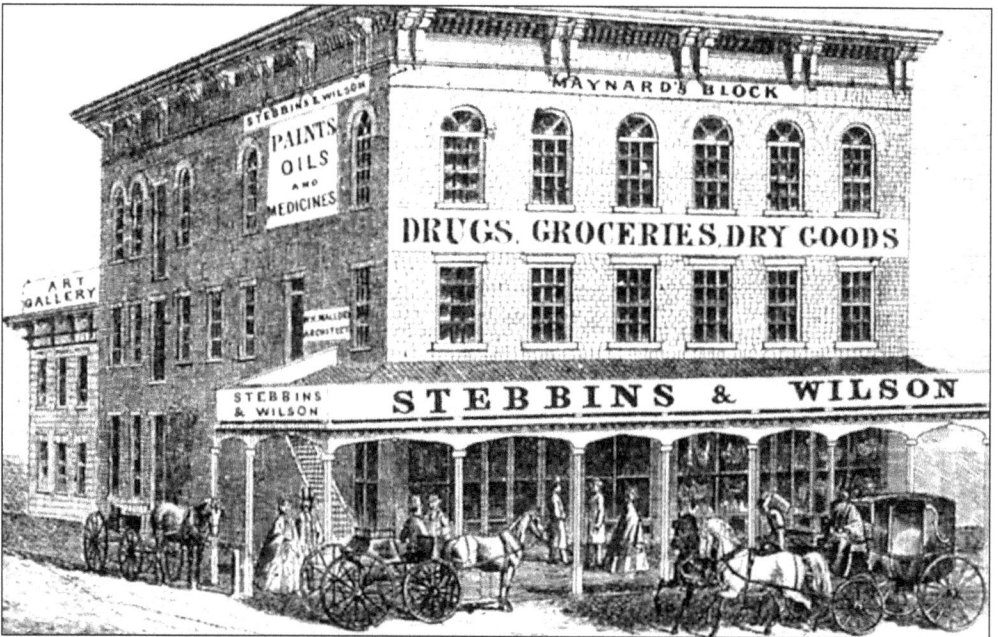

STEBBINS AND WILSON STORE, NORTHWEST CORNER OF ANN AND MAIN, 1864. The Stebbins and Wilson store (another Maynard Block, as he was originally their partner) replaced an older building from Ann Arbor's first decade. Both sold a variety of goods as seen in this engraving from the 1864 *Washtenaw County Plat Map*. It was demolished in 1925 for a gas station, now the Main Street Party Store.

ONE OF
THE FINEST
IN THE STATE

Heated
with
Steam

Lighted
by Gas.

Seating Capacity, - 1,200
Width of Stage, - 60 ft.
Depth of Stage Loft, 30 ft.
Stage to Rigging Loft, 30 ft.
Proscenium Opening, 27 ft.
Height of Flats, - 15 ft.

(FROM PHOTO BY GIBSON)

GRAND OPERA HOUSE.
ANN ARBOR, MICH.

HILL'S OPERA HOUSE, SOUTHWEST CORNER OF MAIN AND ANN, C. 1900. Any town with class had an opera house and George D. Hill, a prominent mill owner, constructed this one in the Second Empire style in 1871. Hill gave his name to Hill Street where he built a remarkable house (also gone). In 1906, two floors were added and it became the Whitney Theater. Live shows featured famous actors of the day. In 1952 it was ordered demolished as a fire hazard and replaced by a parking lot, still there today.

OPERA HOUSE, - - - - ANN ARBOR.

LADIES AND CHILDREN'S

GRAND MATINEE

—BY THE—

Boston Ideal Juvenile Comic Opera Company

Saturday, Feb. 10, at 2.30 P. M.

This Card, with 15 Cents, will Admit any Scholar of the Public Schools to the Matinee. Adults 25 and 35 Cents.

Saturday Evening, at 8, they will appear in their Great Rendering of

PATIENCE.

OPERA HOUSE ADVERTISING CARD, 1880s. Hill's Opera House not only featured important traveling troupes of the day but also had special shows for children. This card, with its myriad ornamental typefaces, is typical of the 1880s.

The Clarken Block Being Demolished, 115 North Main, 1956. George Clarken retired to Ann Arbor in 1872 and made a killing in the grocery business. In 1880 he expanded the old store of John Maynard to designs by architect George Schwab, in order to house various businesses including a billiard hall. It was demolished shortly after the Opera House and also became a parking lot which it remains today.

THE CLARKEN BLOCK LOOKING SOUTH, 115 NORTH MAIN, 1956. Here is another view of the demolition of the Clarken Block showing the streetscape of Main Street looking south across Huron. Notice the road signs for U.S. 12 and U.S. 23 (i.e. Huron St.), indicating the impact of increased traffic on Main Street. The tall building still stands as a recognizable landmark while the corner building is now covered with black granite and is bigger than it was then.

109 SOUTH MAIN, 1856. Guiterman's Clothing store, seen here in an engraving from the *Washtenaw County Plat Map*, was the first of many clothing stores to occupy this building over a 50-year span. The Guiterman brothers were among the earliest Jewish residents in Ann Arbor, most of whom left to join the larger Jewish community in Detroit.

PREKETES SUGAR BOWL, 109 SOUTH MAIN, C. 1940. The Greek-owned Preketes Sugar Bowl opened in 1910 and was a mainstay of downtown as a purveyor of ice cream and sweets until 1960. Greeks began settling in Ann Arbor in the early 20th century to "make a few bucks and go back home and live like kings," as one descendant remembered. They wound up staying, many in the ice cream, candy, and restaurant line. This building was demolished in 1969 for an addition to the corner bank.

23

VIEW OF THE SOUTH SIDE OF THE 100 BLOCK OF EAST HURON, 1932. Another aerial shot taken from the tower of the courthouse looking across Huron shows the downtown panorama beyond. The small buildings between the Allenel Hotel and the Farmers and Mechanics Bank were built in the early decades of Ann Arbor, probably in the 1840s, and have all been demolished. The two tall buildings remain today as the Ypsi-Ann on the left and the First National Bank on the right. The building just to the left of the Allenel also survives as the Embassy Hotel. The Farmers and Mechanics Bank replaced the one destroyed in 1927 by two interurban cars that got loose at the top of the Jackson Avenue hill and barreled into the building one evening. This building was covered in black granite and expanded both to the south and the east in the 1960s.

Two

The 40-Acre University

The original 1837 campus of 40 acres, bounded by State Street and North, South, and East University Streets, was donated by the Ann Arbor Land Company, a group of seven men whose memory has been at least partially perpetuated in street names: Thayer, Ingalls, Maynard, and Thompson. Almost all campus buildings were constructed on this former farmland until the late 19th century. The 20th century saw expansion in a ring around the original 40 acres, leaving a small commercial district at State and North University.

The University didn't open for classes until 1841. The buildings then consisted of a single classroom/dormitory structure and four professors' residences. The campus grew under dynamic presidents Henry Philip Tappan (1852–1863) and James B. Angell (1871–1909). When Angell arrived, the university had nine buildings. He oversaw the addition of 30 more before stepping down. By the turn of the century, the campus was a thicket of structures, most built of red brick in a weighty Renaissance style. The lone survivors from the 19th century are the U-M President's House and Tappan Hall. The loss of Barbour-Waterman Gym in 1977, just one year after the American bicentennial, when old buildings were being enthusiastically celebrated, was the last demolition of a major university building. Reaction to this loss, which was opposed by many and championed by few, led to the listing of the central campus on the National Register of Historic Places.

25

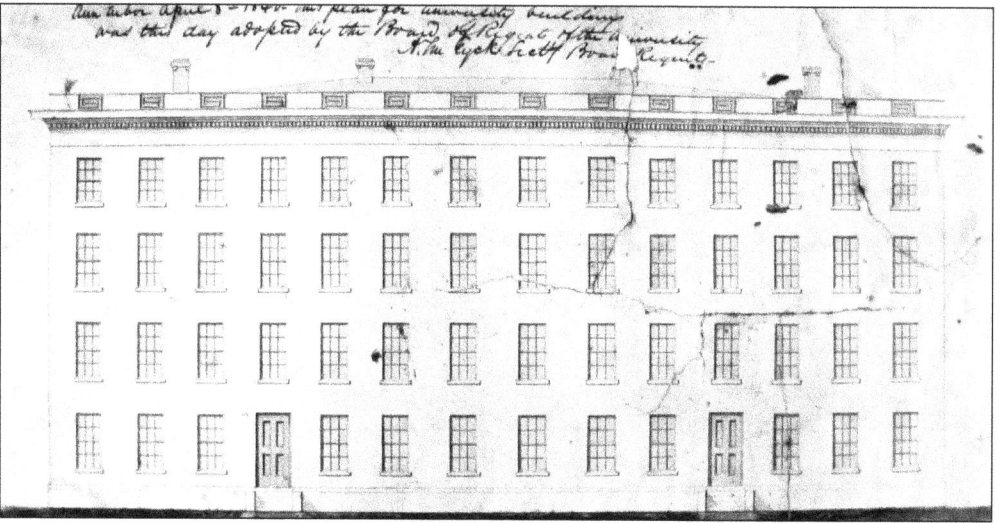

THE ORIGINAL PLAN FOR MASON HALL, 1840. On April 8, 1840, the Regents approved a plan for a main classroom building and work soon began to make the University of Michigan a reality. This simple building was a concession to practicality and to the depressed financial situation of the state, which made it impossible to build the elaborate Gothic Revival plans submitted by Alexander Jackson Davis, famous architect of the day.

MASON HALL AND SOUTH COLLEGE, 1861. Mason Hall opened in 1841 and its twin, later known as South College, opened in 1849. They contained dormitories, classrooms, a chapel, recitation rooms, a library, and a museum. The stucco-over-brick buildings were simple but "well executed" and the cornice "particularly pleases me" wrote a student of Dr. Emil Lorch in 1935.

MAP OF CAMPUS, 1847.
A student of the class of 1847 drew this map from memory many years after his graduation. It shows the original classroom buildings and the four professors' houses. Only one of the houses survives as the President's residence. Latrines and a wood yard were prominent campus features.

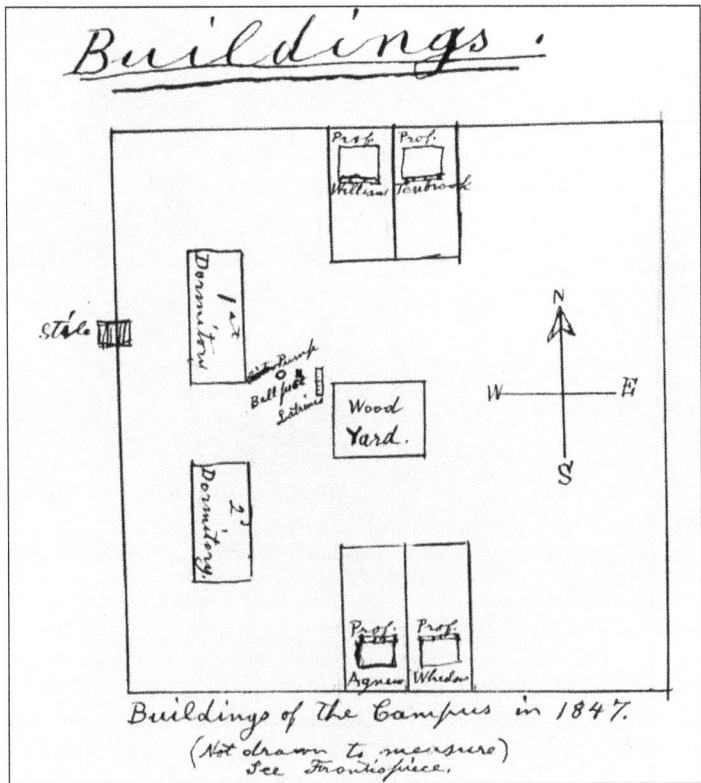

Buildings of the Campus in 1847.
(Not drawn to measure)
See Frontispiece.

1840s PROFESSOR'S HOUSE, NORTH UNIVERSITY, 1876. One of four professors' houses built in 1840, this view shows the northwest house before it was remodeled and still sported its Greek meander pattern along the roof line. It had just become the Dental School but would be the Homeopathic Hospital by 1879. It served as a classroom building for the Homeopathic Medical School until 1914, when it was demolished for the Natural Science (Kraus) Building.

PROFESSOR'S HOUSE AS THE UNIVERSITY HOSPITAL, AFTER 1876. The easternmost house on North University was converted into University Hospital in 1869, the first in the United States. Pavilions of wood were added so that in case of infestation they could be burned down. Additions were made for nurses' quarters and dining facilities. In 1908 it was demolished for the Chemistry Building.

PROFESSOR'S HOUSE ON SOUTH UNIVERSITY, AFTER 1878. A third professor's house built in 1840 on South University, east of the one that became the President's House. It was a house until 1877, after which it became the home of the Dental School (1877–1891), and one of several buildings of the Engineering School (1891–1922). It was demolished in 1922 for the Clements Library.

UNIVERSITY HALL AND DOME UNDER CONSTRUCTION, 1873. In 1871, the cornerstone was laid for University Hall, which linked and subsumed the two original classroom buildings. It too was stucco-over-brick in the Renaissance Revival style. More space was badly needed since enrollment had reached 1,000. "U" Hall had a large auditorium which could hold 3,000 and was used for graduation exercises.

UNIVERSITY HALL, 1877. Designed by Edward S. Jenison of the Engineering Class of 1868, University Hall was a campus landmark for almost 80 years and linked the two original buildings known as Mason Hall and South College. The auditorium had an elliptical balcony that could hold 1,300. Many alumni posed before its stately façade and university events and concerts— open to the public—were held there as well.

UNIVERSITY HALL WITH NEW DOME, 1905. The handsome but leaky dome of University Hall was replaced in 1896 by a humbler affair made of iron and set atop the hall, "much to the disappointment of alumni," according to U-M historian Howard Peckham. By the 1920s, even more classroom space was needed and Angell Hall was erected, entirely blocking this view of the older building.

UNIVERSITY HALL BEING RAZED, 1950. The destruction of Haven Hall by a student arsonist in 1950 precipitated the demolition of the three buildings that formed University Hall in September of 1950. This photo clearly shows how University Hall and Angell were attached. The old cornerstone with Jenison's name on it now rests in a hallway linking Angell Hall with replacement versions of Mason and Haven Halls.

LAW DEPARTMENT BUILDING, 1870S. The Law Department Building (1863), designed by architects Spier and Rohn of Detroit in the Italianate style, stood near the corner of State and North University. The building also housed the University Chapel until 1873 and the General Library until 1883 (both moved from crowded Mason Hall).

UNIVERSITY HALL AND LAW DEPARTMENT BUILDING, C. 1873. Seen here with University Hall, the Law Department Building is surrounded by trees. Also visible are a large boulder placed by the class of 1862 and the ornate portion of the wooden campus fence that served as the main entrance for many years.

LAW DEPARTMENT BUILDING, 1896. The Law Department Building was altered twice, first in 1893 with a tower addition, and again in 1898 when the despised tower was removed and the building was further enlarged. It was renamed Haven Hall in 1933 in honor of former U-M President Erastus O. Haven (1863–1869) after the Law School moved to the Cook Quadrangle at State and South University.

HAVEN HALL DESTROYED BY FIRE, 1950. Michigan Governor G. Mennen "Soapy" Williams, right, his wife Nancy Quirk Williams, and U-M Vice President Robert W. Briggs stand at the wreckage of Haven Hall, destroyed by a student arsonist upset about his grades. After the fire, the Regents and President A.G. Ruthven made an emergency appeal to the State Legislature for funds to demolish University Hall and replace it with new classroom and office space.

CHEMICAL LABORATORY, 1874. At the urging of President Tappan, this building was erected in 1856 as a "Chemical Laboratory for the analytical courses" because he wished to model the University of Michigan on German universities. Tappan was ahead of his time and was fired due to political and sectarian rivalry. Later President Angell would remark that Tappan was "the largest figure of a man that ever appeared on the Michigan campus. And he was stung to death by gnats!"

FIRE DESTROYS THE ECONOMICS BUILDING (FORMER CHEMICAL LABORATORY), 1981. On Christmas Eve 1981, a disgruntled employee set the Economics Building on fire, leaving the building in ruins, with the life's work of many faculty members destroyed. Originally the Chemical Laboratory, the building had been expanded many times—in 1861, 1866, 1868, 1874, 1890, and 1901. Through it all, it retained its character as a pre-Civil War building and was a second home for many Economics faculty.

THE FIRST MEDICAL BUILDING, 1865. At the urging of physicians and surgeons throughout the state, the university opened a Medical Department, and in 1850 built this magnificent structure of sandstone in the style of a Greek temple with a portico and columns topped by Egyptian-Revival capitals. In its time, it was the finest building on campus. In 1864, the addition at the rear of the building was constructed because of a dramatic increase in the number of medical students after the Civil War. The building was given other uses when the "new" medical building was erected in 1904 (now the School of Natural Resources Building). Damaged by fire in 1911, the old landmark was razed in 1914. Randall Lab is on the site today.

FIRST UNIVERSITY LIBRARY, C. 1900. The first free-standing library, with its curved wall reading room, was completed in 1883 and was a beloved campus fixture for decades. Designed by the firm of Ware and VanBrunt, it had a clock tower and chimes that summoned students to class. In 1898 new "stacks" were added, and the original building remodeled. It was declared unsafe in 1915, but the fireproof stacks were preserved and incorporated into the new library.

READING ROOM, UNIVERSITY LIBRARY, C. 1890. The library also served as an art gallery, and this statue of "Michigan" loomed over the scholars as they studied by gaslight. The heroic figure was made by Randolph Rogers (a native of Ann Arbor who became famous as a sculptor in Rome) as a plaster cast for the bronze Soldiers and Sailors Monument in Detroit. Exiled with casts of other Rogers works to the basement of University Hall when the library was demolished, it was destroyed by steam heat. The statue in Detroit is still standing.

35

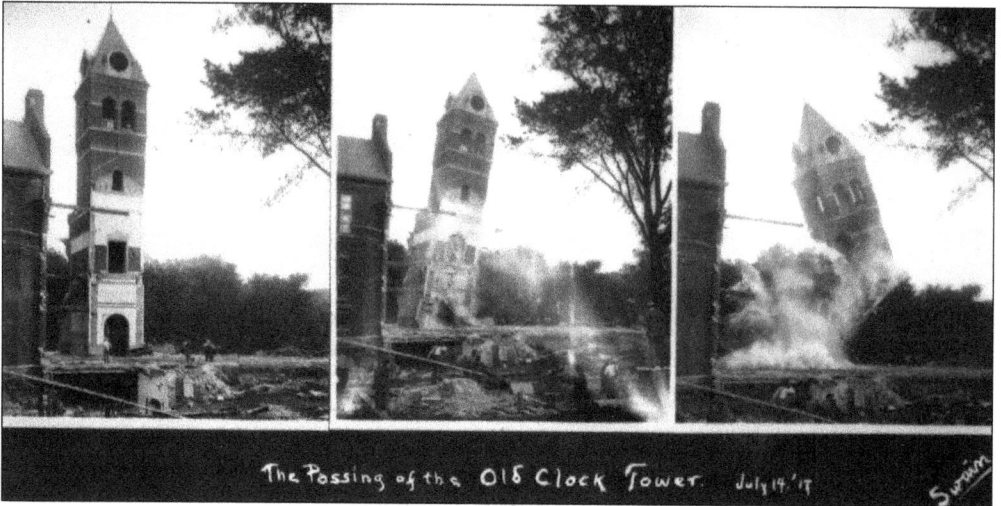

LIBRARY CLOCK TOWER DEMOLITION, 1917. The "passing of the Old Clock Tower" as Ann Arbor photographer George Swain labeled it, was a sad day for many residents and alumni. But the new building that replaced it, the Harlan Hatcher Library designed by renowned Detroit architect Albert Kahn, has proven its staying power. The chimes and clock were moved to the Engineering Laboratory that was eventually demolished as well.

THE ENGINEERING LABORATORY, 1894. An impressive testimonial to the growing importance of the physical sciences, the 1885 Engineering Laboratory was designed in a similar Romanesque style as the library. It was designed by Gordon Lloyd, another renowned Detroit architect famous for his Gothic Revival churches in Ann Arbor. Engineering expanded to the east and eventually moved to North Campus. This building was demolished in 1956 for the Undergraduate (Shapiro) Library.

CENTRAL CAMPUS FROM THE MICHIGAN UNION, 1918. Photographer George R. Swain caught this view looking northeast, with the University Museum in the foreground and the new library under construction behind it. The museum was also a towered landmark, designed in 1879 by William LeBaron Jenney, who had taught architecture at U-M before moving to Chicago where he gained acclaim as the inventor of the skyscraper.

THE MUSEUM, C. 1890. Seen here with University Hall, the museum was a muscular structure in a flamboyant Renaissance style. Storage space was a problem from the beginning, as was shoddy construction that resulted from a lack of funds. In 1928 the collections were moved and the building became Romance Languages. In 1958, it too succumbed to the wrecking ball, and the site is now a grassy lawn, slated to become an addition to the U-M Art Museum.

BARBOUR-WATERMAN GYMNASIUMS, 1904. Waterman Gymnasium (on the right) was built for men in 1894 with contributions from Detroit alumni, especially Joshua W. Waterman. Former Regent Levi Barbour helped pay for a gymnasium for women which opened in 1897, after women's organizations on campus raised a good deal of the money. In 1977, the year after the American bicentennial, a controversial decision was made to demolish the gyms. Opposition developed and "Recycle Waterman Gym" buttons were sported. Their demolition prompted preservationists in 1978 to list the entire central campus on the National Register of Historic Places. The Willard H. Dow Laboratory occupies this site today.

Three

The Town Expands
Around the University

Throughout the 19th and 20th centuries, much of Ann Arbor's growth expanded around the U-M central campus and Main Street. Professors built elegant houses in the latest fashion and had large gardens on big lots on streets bordering the campus. Students required lodging and board, and women (often widows) enjoyed an unusually lucrative role in supplying these needs through rooming houses. Bookstores and other businesses catering to students eventually opened on State Street in the 1880s, slowly moving from their Main Street base which served the "town" (German for the most part), rather than the "gown." By the late 1880s, turreted fraternities marched down State Street and muscled into the turf of the professors' houses. Churches built branches closer to campus to be closer to the students.

Many of these buildings eventually were demolished for university uses. On State Street, Betsy Barbour and Helen Newberry dorms replaced older buildings, as did Newberry Hall (the Kelsey Museum), the LS&A Building, and the Michigan Union. On South University, entire blocks of homes gave way for the Law Quadrangle and the Martha Cook Dormitory. On North University, Hill Auditorium, the Dental School, The League, the Museums Building, and the C.C. Little Building all required demolition of residential properties. Today the university borders are Hill, Huron, Glen, and Division Streets, and these boundries are now under feeling the pressure of imminent expansion.

STATE STREET LOOKING NORTH FROM SOUTH UNIVERSITY, C. 1870. A little girl stands with her doll buggy looking at the photographer in the middle of muddy State Street on a typically drab winter's day. In the distance is the steeple of the recently built (1866) Methodist Episcopal Church. On the right is the Law Department, on the left are faculty houses and the First Ward School, with an attic cupola.

WEST SIDE OF STATE STREET SOUTH OF WILLIAM, C. 1870. In the 1870s, private houses and the First Ward School lined State Street opposite the U-M campus. The school was built in 1862, purchased by U-M in 1901, renamed West Hall and demolished in 1923 and is now the lawn of Betsy Barbour dormitory. The small white house was African-American George H. Jewett's Valet Cleaning Shop which stood until 1916. The Congregational Church, which was dedicated in 1876, replaced the square brick building at the corner.

THE BIBLE CHAIR HOUSE, 444 SOUTH STATE, 1917. The Bible Chair House served as a spot for Bible classes for over 25 years. Various classes were held at 4 p.m. daily. The house was built c. 1870 by Dr. Preston B. Rose, Professor of Chemistry, whose name is forever linked with that of Prof. Silas Douglass in the Douglass-Rose controversy of 1875, when he was accused of embezzling funds from the Chemistry Department. The house was demolished in 1933 for the Staebler gas station.

STAEBLER GAS STATION, STATE AND JEFFERSON, 1933. The sleek Art Deco gas station contrasts sharply with the rusticated Richardsonian style Kelsey Museum from the 1880s. In 1933, it stood at the northwest corner of State and Jefferson (this section of the street now closed). Local architects Woody Woodworth and Douglas Loree, who later designed the Art Deco bus depot on West Huron in 1940, followed the current trend and used porcelain enameled steel. It was demolished c. 1946 for what is now the U-M's LS&A Building, which opened in 1948.

THE OLD MORRIS HOMESTEAD, 504 SOUTH STATE. George S. Morris, Professor of Philosophy and mentor to John Dewey when he lived in Ann Arbor, resided in this house in the 1880s. It remained in the family until 1907. Always referred to as Morris Hall, it was stuccoed and remodeled as the Tea Cup Inn in 1908, then sold to the university in 1922. It housed the university's radio broadcasting studio in the 1930s and was fondly remembered in 1987 by Mike Wallace, noted CBS television journalist. It was demolished in 1946 for the LS&A building.

ZETA PSI FRATERNITY, 512 SOUTH STATE, C. 1900. One of several turreted fraternities along State Street, Zeta Psi remained on the block the longest, into the 1950s. Here it is seen with all its flourishes in a 1910 post card. The house had been built much earlier in a Gothic Revival style and remodeled in 1901 by Koch Brothers, a local construction company, who used it in some of their advertisements. The earlier home had belonged to a professor at the university.

JUDGE THOMAS M. COOLEY HOUSE, 534 SOUTH STATE, 1875. Around 1865, Law Professor Cooley had renowned architect Gordon W. Lloyd design this stone house in a Gothic Revival style which befitted the status of its owner. Cooley served on the Michigan Supreme Court and wrote textbooks on the U.S. Constitution. The building was willed to the university for a Men's Union in 1906, remodeled twice and demolished in 1916 for the Union that stands today.

DEMOLITION FOR U-M UNION, 1916. The Cooley house and that of newspaper editor Elihu Pond were demolished in 1916 to construct the Michigan Union. Viewed from the west and looking towards the campus, one might see these ruins as the community did—as a step forward. Ironically, both of Elihu Pond's were architects and they designed the Michigan Union keeping the old house plan in mind. The Pendleton Room is said to be where the Pond Brothers had their bedroom.

ALPHA DELTA PHI AND CLEMENTS HOUSE, 548 AND 556 SOUTH STATE STREET, C. 1890. These two magnificent turreted buildings stood on the west side of State Street, just south of the intersection with South University. Built in the 1870s and 1880s, one was a fraternity and the other the childhood home of lumber magnate and later Regent William L. Clements (class of 1882), whose fortune built the Clements Library. The Sigma Chi fraternity purchased the Clements house and kept it until 1913, when they built their present Renaissance Revival building.

ALPHA DELTA PHI, C. 1905. Another view of the Alpha Delta Phi fraternity house shows the richness of detail and its complicated rooflines and window variations, all hallmarks of the Victorian era. The fraternity was established at U-M in 1846 and built this structure in the 1880s. It was demolished in 1910 and a "modern" fraternity building, designed by Dean & Dean of Chicago, was built.

VIEW OF SOUTH UNIVERSITY LOOKING EAST, 1920. Looking east in 1920 from the tower of the Michigan Union, we see the site of the future Cook Law Quadrangle. The Martha Cook Dormitory is visible in the background. Within 10 years, none of these buildings would be standing. The round-walled building was the Memorial Christian Church, which was moved and now stands at the corner of Tappan and Hill Street.

PSI UPSILON FRATERNITY HOUSE, 1917. The 1879 Psi Upsilon fraternity house with its towers and turrets stood at the corner of State and South University until the 1920s, when it was demolished for the English Gothic Law Quadrangle. Designed by Chicago architect and former U-M professor William LeBaron Jenney, it was the first fraternity house in Ann Arbor built for that purpose. A June 1923 newspaper noted: "All the work of demolishing the Psi Upsilon house has been completed and the steam shovel will clear away the remainder. . ."

ACACIA FRATERNITY, 603 SOUTH STATE, C. 1920. Founded at the University of Michigan in 1904, the Acacia Fraternity built this Craftsman-style house in 1910 after demolishing an 1870s house on the site. This was torn down for the Cook Law Quadrangle and the fraternity was uprooted to another part of town.

DELTA KAPPA EPSILON FRATERNITY, 609 SOUTH STATE, 1914. The DKE Fraternity, Omicron chapter, was organized in 1855. In 1888 the fraternity built this fieldstone house with a wide veranda and arched entry after demolishing the previous house on the site. This structure was demolished in 1922 for the Law Quadrangle. A 1901 publication described the house as having the "air of a gentlemen's private residence or country club." The fraternity's 1878 clubhouse, the mysterious "Shant," designed by William LeBaron Jenney, still stands at 611 1/2 East William Street.

RESIDENCE OF MRS. WRIGHT, 733 SOUTH STATE, 1893. On the crest of State at Hill Street, this home built by a Mrs. Wright became a fraternity house by 1896. Its Victorian look, with horseshoe arch surrounded by mock Tudor and Swiss designs and polygonal tower, was the height of fashion. It was remodeled by later fraternities and destroyed by arson after it was abandoned by its last occupant, Sigma Phi Epsilon. This is the site of the Gerald Ford School of Public Policy.

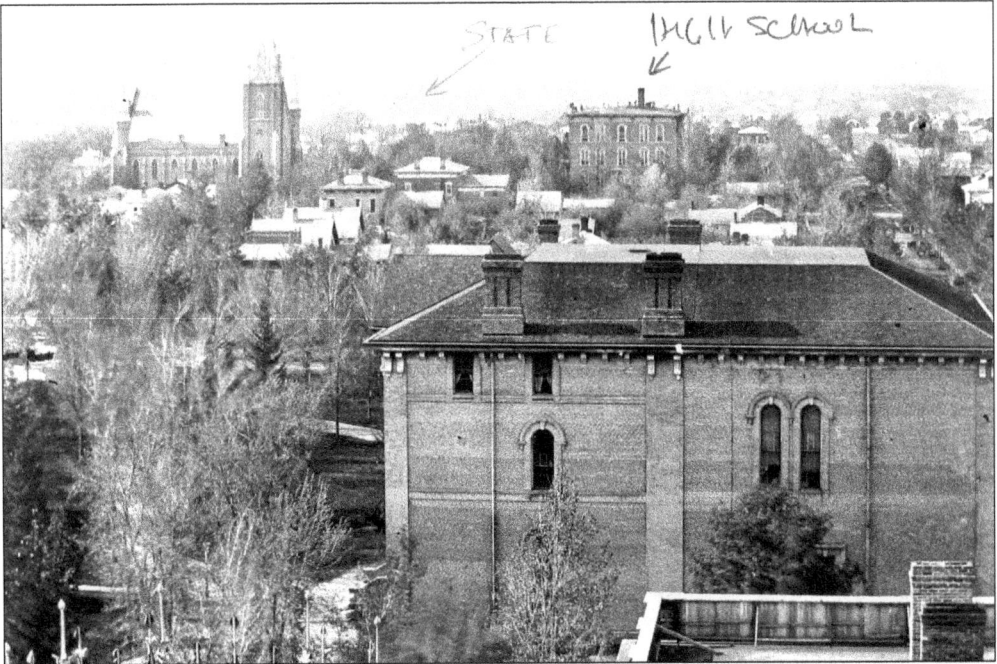

VIEW FROM UNIVERSITY HALL LOOKING NORTH, C. 1880. Large houses on State Street north of North University are glimpsed from above with the spire of the 1866 Methodist Church (at Washington Street) in the upper left, and the arched windows of the Union High School visible to the right of center. In the immediate foreground is the Law Building. Only one of these structures remains today, at 215 South State, behind the Kaleidoscope Bookstore.

PROFESSOR WINCHELL'S OCTAGON HOUSE, NORTH UNIVERSITY, 1870s. Professor Alexander Winchell—who taught physics, engineering, zoology, botany, and geology at various times—built this octagon house in 1858 according to tenets expounded by Squire Orson Fowler, a famous phrenologist and writer on health and happiness. Winchell's house, surrounded by extensive gardens, was sold to a fraternity in the 1890s, then to the U-M in 1909, and razed for construction of Hill Auditorium.

NORTH UNIVERSITY AVENUE, 1870s. North University Avenue, with the tower of Winchell's Octagon visible through the trees, was a boulevard lined with houses and trees in the 1870s. It terminated at the home of Law Professor and Judge William Asa Fletcher, visible in the distance. Fletcher was the first Chief Justice of the Michigan Supreme Court and a U-M Regent. Fletcher Street was named for him in 1935. His former home was used as nurses' quarters until demolished in 1909 for the Museums Annex.

NORTH UNIVERSITY AVENUE, 1914. Commercialization on North University commenced in earnest in the first decades of the 20th century as this photo of Michigan bandsmen and students shows. The Knights Templar, a Masonic organization, are returning from a funeral at Forest Hill Cemetery. Note the trolley tracks on the right.

LYNDON PHOTO SHOP, 717–719 NORTH UNIVERSITY, C. 1915. Two of the new businesses on North University opposite the entry to campus were the Ideal Barber Shop and A.S. Lyndon's Photography Studio, seen in this snowy photo. Lyndon took numerous pictures of university activities and town landmarks and his camera sign was a work of art. He opened in 1905 and claimed to have taken more commercial photographs than any other photographer in the city. This building was destroyed by fire in 1929.

ARCADE THEATER, 715 NORTH UNIVERSITY, 1915. In the middle of the commercial section of North University was the Arcade Theater, which showed silent movies to raucous student audiences. After it burned in 1929, The *Ann Arbor Daily News* conducted a naming contest for a replacement theater, but a building with shops was put on the site instead. It is now occupied by Hamilton Square.

ANN ARBOR SAVINGS BANK BRANCH, 707 NORTH UNIVERSITY, c. 1920. The Ann Arbor Savings Bank opened its doors in 1869 at the corner of Huron and Main. Judge Thomas Cooley helped in the organizing, as did many other citizens. The bank opened its campus branch at 707 North University in the first decades of the 20th century when Main Street merchants opened branches near campus. This lovely, restrained classical building was demolished in 1937 for a Kresge's dimestore, now Michigan Book and Supply.

U-M League Cornerstone Laying, 1928. The U-M Women's League, located on what was once Ingalls Street (now gone), was designed by Ann Arbor-born Chicago architects Pond and Pond, who also designed the Michigan Union built where their father's home had stood. Note the houses on Fletcher Street visible in the background, which were demolished in the next decade for the U-M Health Service Building.

U-M League Construction, 1928. Taken two weeks before the laying of the cornerstone, this photo shows a large house on Ingalls and Hill Auditorium in the background. The League played an important role in the social life of female students for many decades, since they weren't allowed in the Michigan Union without an escort. Many houses were demolished to build the Michigan League.

PRETTYMAN'S BOARDING HOUSE, NORTH UNIVERSITY AND FLETCHER, 1897. Boarding houses flourished near the campus and Prettyman's was one of the most famous. William Lewis Adams' mother wrote on the back of this photograph: "William had his meals here and lived here part of the time." "Prett's" was demolished in 1938 for the Dental School and the *Michigan Alumnus* bemoaned its loss, calling it "one of the triumvirate which reigned at the top in student popularity in Ann Arbor for many undergraduate generations."

STATE STREET LOOKING NORTH, C. 1877. Scholars wearing mortarboards walk towards campus at the corner of State and North University. Commercialization of State Street is now evident. Bookstores were the first to businesses open here (Sheehan's claimed to be the first) and others catering to students opened soon afterwards. The Methodist church looms in the background, a landmark for almost 80 years. Trees indicate that portions of State Street were still residential.

STATE STREET LOOKING NORTH, 1920S. The same scene 50 years later: the trees have vanished (save one elm) as have the houses on the west side of State Street, south of Liberty. Several of the tin-facade buildings at the left have survived, though some had fires and were remodeled. The building cornices were removed long ago. The Methodist church stands tall in the background, not be demolished until 1940.

NICKELS MEAT MARKET, 326 SOUTH STATE STREET, 1890S. In 1868, John H. Nickels opened his meat market on State Street and later became very prosperous. His son Tom also prospered, buying out his siblings and tearing down the old market to build the Nickels Arcade in 1915–1918. The Arcade was listed in the National Register of Historic Places in 1987.

HALL RESIDENCE ON SOUTH UNIVERSITY, C. 1918. Commercial development was not as strong along the South University border of campus, perhaps because the Cousins & Hall greenhouses were at 1002 South University for almost half a century. This 1860s house was the home of John H. Hall Sr. John H. Hall Jr. lived next door. John Sr. noted that when he built his house only one other existed—that of carpenter James Cook. The Martha Cook dormitory is visible in the background.

COUSINS & HALL FLORISTS AND GREENHOUSES, SOUTH UNIVERSITY, C. 1900. Cousins & Hall showcased their wares through glass plate windows. Their busiest season was during Commencement, when they decorated University Hall with flowers and made baskets of cut flowers as gifts for each graduate. The university bought and demolished the two properties in 1918, but the site remained open space until 1998 when the School of Social Work was dedicated. Cousins & Hall built a retail store at 611 East University.

FIRST METHODIST CHURCH, STATE STREET NEAR WASHINGTON LOOKING NORTH, C. 1866. This rare photograph shows the recently-built Gothic-style Methodist church with residential neighbors on the west side of State at the corner of Washington Street. State is a dirt road and horse-drawn wagons were the transport of the day. The house was later moved and Lane Hall was built in its place.

FIRST METHODIST CHURCH C. 1916. In 1915, the house was moved west of its lot (and is still there) and Lane Hall was constructed as the Student Christian Association. Horse and wagon have given way to the car and truck and telephone poles line the street. In 1906 the church steeple was hit by lightning and the burning portion fell into the street, creating a memorable event for many citizens. In 1940, the church was demolished and replaced with a country-Gothic church.

STATE AND HURON LOOKING SOUTH, 1916. Immediately north of the Methodist church were McMillen Hall (1889) and Sackett Hall (1856), buildings of the Presbyterian Campus Ministry. Sackett Hall was a converted home built by Ezra Seaman, but McMillen was erected for religious use. By the 1880s, major Protestant denominations had constructed student ministry buildings near campus, some to keep the impressionable young from attending the nearby Unitarian church. Ann Arbor High School (now the Frieze Building) stood across the street.

GOODRICH HOUSE, 205 SOUTH STATE STREET (SOUTHEAST CORNER OF STATE AND WASHINGTON), C. 1935. Built around 1860, the Goodrich house stood kitty-corner to the Methodist church. Cornelius Goodrich, a pioneer settler, lived here until his death. In 1935 his daughters sold the home to the Michigan Municipal League, which occupied it until 1971, when it was demolished for a restaurant. Its overnight demolition sparked political action, which eventually led to the creation of historic districts. The Corner House Apartments stand at this corner today.

THE UNION HIGH SCHOOL, 100 BLOCK OF SOUTH STATE, 1856. After Ann Arbor became a city in 1851, residents of the four school districts could send their children to one high school (hence the name union), built in 1856 on the east side of State Street between Huron and Washington. It became a magnet for students from all over Michigan as a preparatory school for the University of Michigan. Whole families sometimes moved to the area to send their children to this school. As a result of the increase in enrollment, the school required many additions over the years, some sympathetic to the original design and some not. The only Carnegie library ever attached to another building still stands on East Huron, now part of the Frieze Building.

ANN ARBOR HIGH SCHOOL, 1894. In the 1890s, Ann Arbor High School was a hodgepodge of architectural styles. It was destroyed in a spectacular fire on New Year's Eve 1904, and students and teachers heroically rescued what they could of the library books. A 1,480-pound bell, purchased in 1870, crashed to the ground and broke in two. The memory of that bell didn't die, however. Alumna Lucy Chapin sold tiny souvenir bells made from pieces of the old one. Inscribed on them was "A.A.H.S. 1854–1904." Proceeds supported the W.S. Perry Scholarship Fund. In 1907, a new building was dedicated, designed by the Detroit firm of Malcomson and Higginbotham. In 1955, U-M purchased the building and renamed it after Henry S. Frieze. The Frieze Building remains today.

Four

The Automobile
Conquers Huron Street

In the late 19th century, Ann Arbor's most fashionable residential addresses were on East Huron and North Division (extending east to State Street and north to the Broadway Bridge), clustered near the major Protestant churches. By the mid-20th century, lavish homes on Huron were gone and pretty much forgotten. Only a few remain today to remind us of an earlier era.

The major culprit in the changing face of the town has been the automobile. In the early part of the 20th century, the acceptance of the car over the horse began to accelerate, and by the end of World War I the car-dominated world we know today had arrived. The first concrete road in the U.S. was built in Detroit in 1908, and the first road maps were issued in 1914. In 1921, Jackson Road became U.S. Highway 12 (remaining such until 1956) and in 1923 Ann Arbor passed a zoning ordinance specifying Huron as a commercial corridor; today it is the business route for I-94 and U.S. 23. Down went houses, and up sprang gas stations, at every major intersection. Later came the automobile showrooms, used car lots, and parking lots. Today a few remaining gas stations speak of the early days of our nation's love affair with the automobile. The speed with which the automobile affected the physical landscape is impressive. Like an idea whose time had come, it slashed impediments out if its way, as it made itself indispensable.

HURON AT STATE, LOOKING WEST, C. 1865. In this leafless streetscape, we see some of the mansions that lined East Huron, including the Seaman residence on the left and the Sperry residence on the right. White picket fences were as much to keep animals in, as to give an air of wealth. Emil Lorch referred to the Sperry house as "one of the earliest residences" (1830s). Note in the distance the rise of West Huron Street (Jackson Road) from the bed of Allen Creek.

EZRA SEAMAN HOUSE, HURON AND STATE, 1856. In 1855, *The Washtenaw Whig* reported "Mr. Seaman's house is going up," a year after Seaman arrived in Ann Arbor from Saratoga, New York, where he had his legal training. This variation on the Greek Revival style fitted his stature, both as lawyer and editor/publisher of the *Ann Arbor Journal*, an anti-slavery newspaper. He died in 1879 and later Seaman's daughter Louisa Sackett willed it to the Presbyterians and it became Sackett Hall. It was demolished in 1938 when the new Methodist church was built on this site.

WESTMINSTER HOUSE, 602 EAST HURON, C. 1913. Westminster Home was begun in 1909 by Dr. and Mrs. French as a place to provide housing for Presbyterian female students. Described as a beautiful "colonial" house, it was built in the early 1840s for Professor Fasquelle, chair of the Modern Languages Department, and later inhabited by his daughter, Mrs. Hennequin, whose husband was a Professor of French and German. It was later the home of Dr. George Dock, Professor of Clinical Medicine. It was demolished for the Wesley Foundation in 1940.

LEWIS RISDON RESIDENCE, 607 EAST HURON, 1874. Lewis Risdon, a hardware dealer with a store on Main Street, was successful enough to build this high-style Italianate brick house around 1868. Troubles must have beset him, for by 1883 it was the home of Chauncey Millen, a "fancy dry goods" merchant on Main Street. By the early 20th century, the home had been demolished for a dance hall (and later bowling alley), which in turn was demolished in 1965 for the Campus Inn.

RES. OF L.C. RISDON.

REV. GILLESPIE RESIDENCE, 613 EAST HURON, 1930S. Rev. George D. Gillespie, rector of St. Andrew's Episcopal Church, called this Greek Revival confection home from 1861 through 1874. It was probably constructed in the early 1850s. The elaborate porch dates from the 1860s. Professor J.W. Langley later lived here, as did John S. Nowland, son of a pioneer family. It is now the location of the Campus Inn parking lot.

AUGUSTUS JAYCOX HOUSE, 503 EAST HURON, C. 1870. Ann Arbor at one time was filled with elaborate Second Empire homes (the mansard roof is a hallmark of the style) but few remain today. This beauty was the home of a "Southern Colonel" and liquor distiller who "used it for a fashionable residence for 20 years," according to an article in the Ann Arbor News. It was later remodeled with elaborate porches to be more in style.

JAYCOX HOUSE AS BAPTIST STUDENT GUILD, 503 EAST HURON, C. 1940. From 1904 to 1941 Jaycox's remodeled house was known as Tucker Hall, a residence for Baptist students, much like Westminster House across the street. The Baptists claimed that it was the first university student guild house in the nation. In 1946 it became the Red Coach Inn and "took on a colonial motif," according to the *Ann Arbor News*. Herb Estes Ford demolished it in 1950 for a used car lot and today it is the site of Sloan Plaza.

MILES-SINCLAIR-ROGERS-SHEEHAN HOUSE, 417 EAST HURON, C. 1910. This home was built in 1842 by George Miles and enlarged in the 1870s by William Sinclair, a successful miller whose mill was on Broadway. He left for Chicago but returned a broken man, forced to sell his house to lawyer Henry Rogers. Later it was the home of book dealer James V. Sheehan whose shop was the first bookstore on State Street. The house was measured and photographed in 1938 by a student of architecture professor Emil Lorch.

63

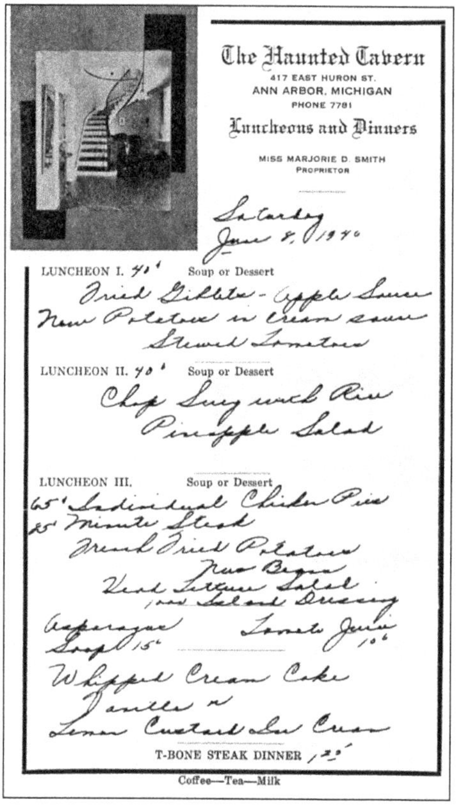

The Haunted Tavern
417 EAST HURON ST.
ANN ARBOR, MICHIGAN
PHONE 7781
Luncheons and Dinners
MISS MARJORIE D. SMITH
PROPRIETOR

Saturday
June 8, 1940

LUNCHEON I. 40¢ Soup or Dessert
Fried Giblets - Apple Sauce
New Potatoes in Cream sauce
Stewed Tomatoes

LUNCHEON II. 40¢ Soup or Dessert
Chop Suey with Rice
Pineapple Salad

LUNCHEON III. Soup or Dessert
65¢ Individual Chicken Pie
85¢ Minute Steak
French Fried Potatoes
New Beans
Head Lettuce Salad
1000 Salad Dressing
Asparagus Soup 15¢ Tomato Juice 10¢
Whipped Cream Cake
Vanilla &
Lemon Custard Ice Cream

T-BONE STEAK DINNER 1.25
Coffee—Tea—Milk

HAUNTED TAVERN MENU, 417 EAST HURON, 1940. In 1930, Sheehan's residence became the Haunted Tavern Restaurant, run by Miss Marjorie Smith. The menu shows the lovely staircase which graced the entry. The house was demolished in 1938 for an A&P grocery store as the new owner, Mr. Thompson of Ypsilanti, said it was "so old that no other use for it could be found." That building survives, much altered, as U-M offices.

FAWCETT HOUSE, 407 EAST HURON (NORTHEAST CORNER OF HURON AND DIVISION), C. 1929. Built in 1895, with a fanciful onion dome, the home of John Travis, publisher of the *Ann Arbor Courier*, dominated the corner of Huron and Division. It later became a sorority and then a restaurant in 1927. Ads stated it was located "where U.S. 12 turns." Despite their famed frog leg dinners, it lasted only three years. The house was demolished for a gas station in 1933. Today much altered, the gas station has become a pizza parlor.

CARROW-MCLEAN HOUSE, 345 EAST HURON C. 1935. On the northwest corner of Huron and Division stood the 1880s home of Dr. Fleming Carrow, professor of ophthalmic and aural surgery. Later it would house Dr. McLean's offices. In 1911, the Knights of Columbus bought it for their clubhouse, selling in 1926 to the Michigamme Oil Company. In 1980, the Issa family opened the Big Market in a newer building, today Ahmo's restaurant.

EAST HURON STREET AND FIRST PRESBYTERIAN CHURCH, C. 1865. Ann Arbor Presbyterians built their third church at the southwest corner of Huron and Division in 1862, here seen with the steeple still missing. Organized in 1826, they were the first church west of Detroit in the Michigan Territory. It was demolished in 1935 to make way for the Ann Arbor News. Beams and bricks from this church were used the same year to build the St. Nicholas Greek Orthodox Church on North Main Street.

65

FIRST PRESBYTERIAN CHURCH, HURON AND DIVISION, 1893. Here is the church as it looked after the steeple was completed. It was made of red brick in a "pointed Gothic" style, popular in the mid-19th century, but unpopular in the 20th. In 1938 the Presbyterians moved into their new church in the "cottage Gothic" style on Washtenaw Avenue where they remain.

LADIES LIBRARY, 324 EAST HURON, 1885. Irving K. Pond of the firm of Pond & Pond of Chicago, whose family owned the *Michigan Argus* (a weekly newspaper), and who lived briefly up the street near State, made these drawings for the Ladies Library Association. Designed in the popular Richardsonian Romanesque style, this building was later home to the Boy Scouts before demolition in 1946 for Michigan Bell Telephone. A limestone Art Deco building occupied the site until the 1970s when it was replaced by the current telephone building.

THE E.W. MORGAN HOUSE, NORTHEAST CORNER OF HURON AND FIFTH AVENUE, C. 1910.
Lawyer Elijah Morgan and his wife Lucy came to Ann Arbor from New York in 1830 and built
this house around 1856. The simple stucco-over-brick house is indicative of their Yankee roots.
Morgan was one of the donors of some of the 40 acres for the original University of Michigan
campus. His house was demolished for a gas station in 1925 and that, in turn, was torn down in
1960 for construction of Ann Arbor's City Hall.

NORTHEAST CORNER OF HURON AND FIFTH AVENUE, C. 1940. By 1940, every intersection
along East Huron between Main and State had at least one gas station, if not several. The
Morgan house was replaced by this station, on the left, built by Standard Oil as the first drive-
in station in town. Previous houses on the street had converted their front yards into business
establishments. One of the best known was the Rentschler Photographic Studio.

THOMPSON-KINNE HOUSE, SOUTHEAST CORNER OF HURON AND FIFTH AVENUE, C. 1910. Built in the 1840s, this interesting variation on Greek Revival style was originally the home of pioneer William R. Thompson. Thompson was another New Yorker who arrived in Ann Arbor in the 1830s. He was also one of the developers who donated the land for the 40-acre campus. It was later the home of Edward D. Kinne, Judge of the Circuit Court for 30 years and mayor from 1875 to 1877. Kinne, too, was a New Yorker and came to Ann Arbor in 1840 to attend the university. He died in 1921 and soon a gas station replaced his home. Today it is a parking lot.

HURON STREET IN 1872, LOOKING SOUTHEAST. This stereocard shows the old fire station at lower left, steeples of the Presbyterian, Baptist, and Methodist churches at upper left, the dome of University Hall at upper right, the steeple of the Congregational church, and the businesses along the south side of the 200 block of East Huron. No building in this photo survives except for a portion of the three-story commercial building.

ANN ARBOR CITY HALL, SOUTHEAST CORNER OF HURON AND FIFTH, 1940. Fifth Avenue demarcated residential from the commercial in 1907, when Ann Arbor's Flemish-style City Hall was erected at the juncture of the two. The common council held meetings upstairs and the police were in the back. Local architect Herman Pipp, a member of the council, designed it. It outgrew the needs of an expanding city and was demolished in 1963 for the City Center Building. Today's City Hall is kitty-corner from the old one.

HURON STREET AT MAIN, LOOKING EAST, 1925. Cars are even more noticeable at this intersection pictured in the early 1950s. The large bank building at the corner is one of two buildings that survive today, but has additions both east and south and has been covered in black granite. In the distance is the steeple of the Presbyterian Church. The tall sign labeled "hotel" marks the other surviving building, which is today the Embassy Hotel.

SOUTHWEST CORNER OF HURON AND FOURTH AVENUE, LOOKING SOUTHWEST, 1930. A panoramic view shows the Allenel Hotel and its dominance of this corner. Cars are evidence that Huron had become a major thoroughfare. Across the street (not in the picture) is the old Washtenaw County Courthouse. Still recognizable are the First National Building (left) and the Glazier Building(right) in the background. The smaller buildings were demolished by mid-century for parking lots and the bank expansion. The Allenel was demolished in 1964 and replaced by a Sheraton Inn, which opened in 1967. In much altered form, that building survives as the Courthouse Square Apartments.

Five

Main Street is the Heart of Downtown

With government functions centered at Main and Huron, it was logical that businesses would develop along Main Street in both directions. After settlement in 1824, Ann Arbor grew quickly. The Erie Canal opened in 1825 connecting Albany with Buffalo, and bringing new settlers (mostly Yankees) into Michigan Territory. When the university opened in 1841, the population was over 2,000. By 1913, it had reached almost 15,000.

Wooden business "blocks" went up quickly to house professional offices and retail stores; these either burned or were torn down in the 1860s for more substantial brick blocks. Built in the Commercial Italianate style, several remain today (without cornices, alas) but many do not. They housed department stores, bakeries, hardware stores, grocery stores, bookstores, and saloons. Corsets and hats were sold opposite beer and brats. Some blocks of Main Street at both the north and south ends remained residential until the late 20th century. A lively mixture of goods and services flourished for over a century. Today, restaurants and art galleries predominate.

LOOKING SOUTHWEST FROM THE COURTHOUSE TOWER, 1893. The courthouse tower was a great vantage point for photography. This view shows the west side of Main Street between Huron and Liberty. The only surviving building in these two blocks is the one in the center, which for decades housed the beloved department store, Goodyear's, and is often called the Goodyear's Block, along with Muehlig's, at the corner. In 1984 the façade was meticulously restored to its original appearance. Some smaller buildings may survive behind radical façade remodelings.

HANGSTERFER'S HALL, SOUTHWEST CORNER OF MAIN AND WASHINGTON, 1869. Jacob Hangsterfer, a German immigrant from Swabia, erected this elaborate Italianate building (with a third floor ballroom) in 1860 and for over 50 years it served as a recreational center. Chapman's 1881 *History of Washtenaw County* notes "as a confectioner, none stood higher in Southern Michigan and his candies were noted far and wide for their excellence and purity." The building was demolished in 1925 and replaced by a Kresge dimestore. Today it is the site of B.D.'s Mongolian Barbecue.

WASHINGTON STREET AT MAIN, LOOKING EAST, C. 1910. Streets were paved with brick by 1910, and cars were slowly beginning to replace horses. Hoag's "Home Store" followed in a long line of clothing stores that occupied the southeast corner, beginning in the 1860s with Joe T. Jacobs. In the distance are steeples of the Lutheran and Methodist churches. Hoag's was demolished in 1926 for the First National building. The bank on the corner, previously the site of Eberbach Hardware, is buried under layers of modern siding. The turreted building in the center survives today as a restaurant.

ADVERTISING CARD, ROUND OAK STOVES, EBERBACH HARDWARE, C. 1880. Eberbach's hardware store was a fixture on the northeast corner of Main and Washington for half a century. These large stoves were a specialty. The store was demolished in 1908 for the State Savings Bank building, now covered with dark reflective siding but still housing a bank. The Eberbachs were in the drug business also, and their company still exists today as a manufacturer of electromechanical laboratory products.

SOUTHEAST CORNER OF MAIN AND WASHINGTON, C. 1925. Local photographer Oscar F. Buss shot this scene when buildings in the preceding photograph were beginning to be demolished, showing more cars and no horses. A new light terracotta building housed the First National Bank when it opened in 1929 and claimed to be Ann Arbor's first skyscraper. The building survived, despite opening only months before the stock market crash which heralded the Great Depression.

MAIN STREET AT LIBERTY, LOOKING NORTH, 1893. Trolley tracks, a trolley car, and telephone poles dominate this scene with rows of commercial Italianate buildings from the 1860s and 1870s lining both sides of Main Street between Huron and Liberty. Most of the buildings on the right survive. Only one on the left survives today, now home of the Peaceable Kingdom.

HORN HOTEL, 117 WEST WASHINGTON, C. 1880. Horn and Hoffstetter, masons, ran their business from this "hotel" at 2 West Washington, which was later a grocery store and saloon. A rare tintype shows members of the Heinrich Horn family, immigrants from Swabia, Germany, by way of Ontario, Canada. The Horns left Ann Arbor for Detroit in the 1880s but other family members remained, with familiar names like Muehlig and Volz. The picture is reversed but if it were correct, today's Earle Building would be on the right and another short brick building on the left. The current structure at 117 West Washington was altered after a fire destroyed the third floor c. 1931.

MACK & CO. DEPARTMENT STORE, NORTHWEST CORNER OF MAIN AND LIBERTY, 1930s.
"Mack's" Department Store dominated the retail scene on Main Street for about 80 years. It sold everything, from furniture and clothing, to carpets and silverware. It even had its own pharmacy and bank. In 1860, Christian Mack, another Swabian immigrant, founded Mack & Schmid with his brother-in-law Frederick Schmid Jr.; they split in 1895 and it became Mack & Co. The store closed in 1940 and most of the building was demolished shortly afterwards.

CORSET AD FROM MACK & SCHMID, 1880s. A lovely lady models the latest in corsets on a trade card issued by Mack & Schmid. Cards such as these were colorful and collectible and every business issued them to drum up customers. Corsets were particularly common on these cards. A large corset-making industry developed after the Civil War. The Pratt Building at 306 South Main was actually built as a corset factory.

DEMOLITION OF MACK & CO., 214–218 SOUTH MAIN, 1940. The Depression weakened the company and it closed for good in 1940. Most of the building was demolished except for one section on the left that now houses a poster and framing shop. It was replaced by a Woolworth's dimestore. The corner portion was reduced to one story and remodeled into a Cunningham's Drugs utilizing porcelain enamel panels. This now houses the Parthenon Restaurant. When the panels were removed a few years ago, the building's true age was revealed.

FIRE AT MACK & CO. STORE, SOUTHWEST CORNER OF MAIN AND LIBERTY, 1899. On May 15, 1899, fire badly damaged the furniture division of Mack & Co. The building did survive but was completely remodeled and still stands at this corner. Their building across the street allowed links to the Schwaben Halle on Ashley, where staff were instructed on courteous behavior to customers. At one time Ann Arbor had three large department stores, one on each block on Main, including Mack's, Goodyear's, and Kline's.

HENRY BINDER HOUSE, SOUTHEAST CORNER OF MAIN AND LIBERTY, C. 1868. By the 1860s, commercial buildings began to encroach on residential sections of South Main, and Binder's house was soon to bite the dust. By 1871 he'd built two such commercial buildings, and one housed his saloon and "orchestian" hall, now 301 South Main. His wife and 10 children lived on the upper floors. In this photo, the buildings at 305 and 309 South Main are seen when they were new.

KLINE'S DEPARTMENT STORE WINDOW, 306–310 SOUTH MAIN, C. 1930. Kline's Department Store at 306–310 S. Main opened for business in 1929 and was the last department store on Main Street to close in 1994. It was part of a Midwestern chain and managed to survive competition from Briarwood Mall for over 20 years. This image shows a typical shop window from the early 1930s, when cloche hats which were the rage.

WILLIAM S. MAYNARD HOUSE, NORTHWEST CORNER OF MAIN AND WILLIAM, 1866. W.S. Maynard, land developer and three-term mayor, built a smaller home at this corner as early as 1840. In 1859 it was raised to two and one-half stories and embellished in the latest Italianate manner with a widow's walk and posts shaped like Grecian urns. It was most famous for its broad sweep of lawn that extended half the block, with strutting peacocks and beautiful flowerbeds. Maynard was one of Ann Arbor's earliest settlers and Maynard Street is named for him.

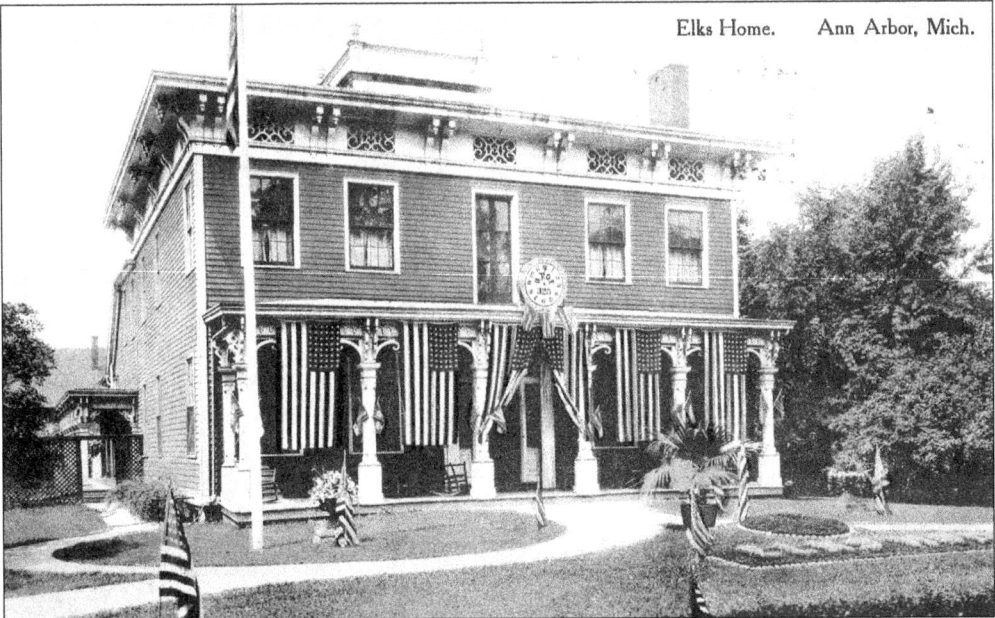

MAYNARD'S HOUSE AS THE ELKS' HOME, C. 1918. Maynard died in 1866 and his second wife in 1888, after which the house was sold and used for 20 years as a hotel, until the Elks acquired it for their lodge. Remodeled almost beyond recognition, first by the Elks and later by Ann Arbor Civic Theater, it was demolished in 1989 and replaced with a large office building. Surviving cornice brackets were rescued and placed on the cornice at 111 West Liberty.

79

MUEHLIG HOUSE, 311 SOUTH MAIN, 1910. German immigrant Florian Muehlig arrived in Ann Arbor in 1840 and began a cabinetry and coffin business in 1852. The company eventually expanded into the funeral home business which still exists under the Muehlig name today. Florian Meuhlig built this home in the 1840s. It was demolished in 1929 by his son, Edward, who opened a hardware store at the site under the name Muehlig & Lanphear.

RED CROSS PARADE, MAIN NEAR WILLIAM, 1918. On Armistice Day, the Red Cross paraded on Main Street and photographer George Swain was there to capture the scene. Behind the marchers is the east side of the 300 block of Main Street. The residential character of half of the block is still much in evidence. It won't be long until the houses disappear, and the march of commerce surges to William Street and beyond.

PHILIP BACH HOUSE, 424 SOUTH MAIN, C. 1930. Philip Bach—German immigrant, dry goods merchant, and former mayor—bought this brick Greek Revival house in 1864 from the Becker family. It was probably constructed in the 1840s. Bach added the Italianate style "piazza" with jig-sawn capitals shortly after purchasing it. In the early 1930s, Bach's daughter Ellen Botsford Bach sold the house to Staebler Oil, and in this image that company has begun to convert it for their use. Today it is the site of Ashley Mews.

BACH HOUSE AS STAEBLER OIL GAS STATION, C. 1935. By 1935, the old landmark had been converted to a full-fledged gas station with a two-bay garage and numerous gas pumps. The brick was covered with stucco and painted, a treatment more common in 1850 than 1930. A former mayor of Ann Arbor, Bach also served on the school board and as a bank vice president. Bach School was named after him. His third wife, Anna Botsford Bach, was an activist in her own right and helped organize the local chapter of the Daughters of the American Revolution.

STAEBLER OIL (FORMER BACH HOUSE) AND SCHMID HOUSE, 424 AND 428 SOUTH MAIN, C. 1935. Staebler Oil sold Dixie Gasoline here and at its other gas stations in town (see page 41). Next door was the home of the famous Rev. Frederick Schmid, built in the 1880s, probably replacing an earlier structure. His son, Frederick Jr., was a partner in Mack & Schmid, whose store was nearby. The residential character of this block was obliterated in the 1980s when two surviving houses were moved to Huron Parkway and converted to medical offices.

SCHLANDERER HOMESTEAD, 504 SOUTH MAIN, 1937. This tiny structure was typical of German immigrant housing. Built in 1862 by the Haupt family, it was sold to the Schlanderers in 1867. A descendant remembered that they'd had to live in the basement when they needed to rent the upstairs. In 1937, a student of Professor Emil Lorch researched and photographed the house. It was moved in 1950 and remodeled beyond recognition. The site became a used car lot.

WEST HURON NEAR FIRST, LOOKING EAST, C. 1932. A political parade with the Boy Scouts in the lead is trying to drum up votes for "McCalla for Sheriff." The photograph also shows the business district on West Huron with the courthouse tower looming in the background. Most of the buildings in this picture are gone, excepting the house on the left and the gas station at the corner (hidden by trees), which is now the Relaxation Station. At one point there were a hotel and a movie theater in the first block of West Huron just west of Main. These were demolished for the parking lot currently at Main and Ashley.

OLD JAIL, 637 NORTH MAIN, 1937. In 1837, the citizens of Washtenaw County hired John and Robert Davidson to build a jail and sheriff's residence on the outskirts of town, four blocks north of the courthouse. It was a stucco-over-brick Greek Revival building with the front used for the sheriff's residence and the rear the actual jail. At the time, it was considered a very handsome building. A hundred years after its construction, it was studied by another of Professor Lorch's students, and viewed as a good example of the Greek Revival style in the Midwest. It was researched, measured, and photographed. In 1885, a third county jail was built on Ann Street and the sheriff, John J. Robison, purchased this one and, tore down the back portion, using the bricks to erect three residences on North Main. Robison continued to occupy the residential portion. Like the Bach house, which it resembles, it too was converted to a gas station in the 1920s. The building was demolished in 1958 after being damaged by a 1951 fire. The Ann Arbor Community Center now stands here.

Six

The Town Expands

Wealth and prosperity accompanied expansion of the university and the boom times after the Civil War. New office blocks (groups of stores built by one developer), houses, churches, and schools went up all over town, and new municipal buildings were constructed to meet the demands of an expanding population. Only a handful of Ann Arbor's earliest municipal buildings survive.

Today it is hard to imagine that South Fourth Avenue, South Fifth Avenue, East Washington, East Liberty, and Maynard were entirely residential areas. Today only Liberty Street contains some houses dating to the 19th century, an anachronistic respite from hard-edged commercial structures in either direction. But they've lost the large lots and the gardens and trees that characterized these streets in the 19th century. They are commonly covered with siding, hiding their Victorian details under armor of aluminum and asphalt. But wonderful examples of Greek Revival, Second Empire, Italianate, and Queen Anne houses were once scattered throughout the central business district.

VIEW FROM THE COURTHOUSE LOOKING SOUTHEAST, C. 1917. George Swain took many photographs from the Courthouse tower and this one shows University Hall and the University Library off in the distance. To their left is the recently built Hill Auditorium, and in the foreground is the Cornwell Coal Company, whose coal heated most of the buildings in town. Right of center is the steeple of Zion Lutheran Church, at the northeast corner of Fifth and Washington.

ZION LUTHERAN CHURCH, NORTHEAST CORNER OF FIFTH AVENUE AND WASHINGTON, c. 1875. In 1875, the recently organized Zion Lutheran congregation purchased and renovated the original building of the First Congregational Church, erected in 1849. Many anti-slavery meetings were held here in the 1850s. In 1893, Zion replaced this church with the one in the photograph above. It too was demolished in 1963 for a bank. Today, Bank of Ann Arbor is located at this corner.

ST. THOMAS THE APOSTLE SCHOOL, ELIZABETH AND KINGSLEY, C. 1896. In 1886, the congregation of St. Thomas built this Romanesque-style school before constructing the present church in 1898. At that time, the church was across the street on Kingsley in a small brick structure built in 1845. The congregation was growing, as German and Italian Catholics joined the primarily Irish congregation. The school was demolished and replaced in 1930 by an Art Deco school on the same site.

JONES SCHOOL (FIRST WARD), 401 NORTH DIVISION, C. 1909. The First Ward School, named Jones School after Elisha Jones, second superintendent of schools, was built in 1869 to accommodate the growth in the school population after the Civil War. By 1920, its six rooms could no longer hold all the children in the district. It was demolished and replaced in 1922 by a second Jones School, now the site of Community High, established in 1973.

MRS. CHARLES BEHR HOUSE, NORTHWEST CORNER OF WILLIAM AND FOURTH AVENUE, 1874. Many elaborate homes were built downtown in the 1870s by successful businessmen. Mrs. Behr's husband, a German immigrant from Swabia, prospered in the grocery business, but died in 1871, leaving her with four children and this lovely Italianate house. In 1927, Ann Arbor Buick announced the formal opening of its used car sales rooms that replaced this home. Today it is the location of the massive Fourth and William parking structure.

CHRISTIAN MACK HOUSE, NORTHEAST CORNER OF WILLIAM AND FOURTH AVENUE, 1940. In 1885, Mack & Company owner Christian Mack built this Second Empire home. In 1914 it was purchased by the YWCA and used as a boarding house for women, with reading rooms, classrooms, and an employment bureau. When the local YMCA and YWCA merged in 1956, the house was demolished for a new "Y" Building. At the right is the parsonage of Trinity Church, also demolished for the new "Y."

PILGRIM HALL, WILLIAM NEAR MAYNARD, C. 1950. Used as a parish house by the First Congregational Church from 1925 to 1950, this 1860s house was previously occupied from 1882 to 1914 by Dr. Sophia Meindermann Hartley, a graduate of the U-M Medical School. Dr. Hartley was one of the city's first female physicians. The structure was demolished in 1950 and today the Congregational Church's Douglas Memorial Chapel occupies this site.

BEAL HOUSE, NORTHEAST CORNER OF WILLIAM AND FIFTH AVENUE, 1890S. In 1867, this lovely high Italianate house was the home of publisher Rice Beal and his adopted son Junius, who became a U-M Regent. Junius also served on the school board and helped organize the interurban railroad. The home was never remodeled and gas fixtures could be found in every room. The plants in the garden were so unusual that U-M students used it for classes. It was demolished in 1956 for the Ann Arbor Public (now District) Library.

FREDERICK SCHMID JR. HOUSE, 438 SOUTH FIFTH AVENUE, 1874. Schmid paid to have this engraving of his home appear in the 1874 *Washtenaw County Atlas* as a symbol of his success. In partnership with his brother-in-law in the firm of Mack & Schmid since 1860, he could afford this Italianate home just down the street from the Beals. The house was demolished in 1924 and replaced with a more modern house which was occupied by a Schmid until 2003.

J.C. WATTS HOUSE, NORTHEAST CORNER OF DIVISION AND LIBERTY, 1932. In 1858, English immigrant and jeweler J.C. Watts built this Italianate home. He lived in it for over two decades. From 1908 to 1945 it was the home and office of Dr. Jeanne C. Solis, one of the few female doctors in Ann Arbor. It later became a furniture store and was demolished in 1953 for Ann Arbor Federal Savings. TCF bank still occupies the site today.

METHODIST CHURCH, SOUTHWEST CORNER OF ANN AND FIFTH AVENUE, C. 1900. The Methodists built their first church here in 1838 and remained until 1866 when they moved to State Street. This building was then used for the Unitarian Church until 1882. The former church was converted to apartments in the early 20th century and was known as the Unity Block. It was demolished in 1935 and remained a parking lot until the fire department built its new headquarters here in 1974. Note the residences of the 300 block of Ann and Catherine in the distance.

333 AND 335 EAST ANN STREET, C. 1935. Mullison's Stables were on East Ann at the turn of the century. In this image, some students from the U-M Riding Club pose after a ride in the snow. The house on the left dates from the 1860s and was the home of Ann Eliza Kellogg. From 1896 to 1905 it was the home of Dr. Carl Huber, professor in the U-M Medical School. The house was demolished around 1954 and replaced with a brick four-flat. The house on the right survives.

91

DANFORTH AND ROYCE HOUSES, NORTHEAST CORNER OF ANN AND FIFTH AVENUE, C. 1875. In 1845, attorney-at-law George Danforth built his Greek Revival home at this corner. In 1866, retired cabinetmaker James Royce built his Italianate home next door at 311 East Ann. The Royce house still stands, divided into apartments but remarkably intact. Danforth's "pleasant" home was used in 1861 to help organize the Soldier's Aid Society for Civil War Relief. It was stucco-over-brick, scored to look like stone, and thus resembled many early U-M buildings and other fine houses in Ann Arbor. In 1968 it was considered for purchase by the Washtenaw County Historical Society for a museum. By the 1950s, it had become a run-down hotel known as the Town House, but its historical importance had not been forgotten. It was demolished in 1971 after partially collapsing. The site has been a parking lot ever since.

LOOMIS HOUSE, 327 EAST ANN STREET, C. 1910. In the 1840s, William Loomis, grocer and partner with Volney Chapin in a foundry, built this Federal-style house between Division and Fifth Avenue. Loomis prospered but his house was partially destroyed by a fire in the early 20th century. The portion on the right survived and was remodeled into a Dutch Colonial house which still stands at 331 East Ann.

FIFTH AND LIBERTY, LOOKING NORTH, 1963. Ann Arbor looked like a sleepy town when Mel Ivory shot this view down South Fifth Avenue. On the left is the former Varsity Laundry, demolished in 1976 for the Federal Building. Across Liberty Street was the beloved Fischer Pharmacy in the Darling Block. The drive-in cleaner's—for a short time, the Sun Bakery—was demolished in 1984 for the 301 East Liberty Building. The portion of the Darling Block that housed the pharmacy survives today as the Afternoon Delight restaurant.

Rettich's Orchestrian Hall, East Washington Near Main, 1874. Rettich was so proud of his new Orchestrian Hall that he paid to have it prominently featured in the 1874 *Washtenaw County Atlas*. The name, however, was just a fancy word for a saloon (with an assemblage of musical instruments playing tunes automatically). Saloons had been on this site since the 1850s and Rettich's remained for decades, after which it became Gustav Brehm's "The Ortman." The Ortman was one of four saloons singled out in an 1898 newspaper article on the dives attended by University students. "This place is used for a regular Sunday drunk by the students and the old woman who keeps it sees nothing and sells the boys keys for $1, to visit with women of questionable character," wrote a journalist of the *New York Voice*. The Anti-Saloon League kept watch on the 89 saloons in the city one night and reported 500 students there. Eventually the League won the battle (but lost the war), and the building became a barber shop, print shop, and men's clothing store. By the 1960s, it had been incorporated into a bank.

NORTHWEST CORNER OF FOURTH AVENUE AND WASHINGTON, 1907. The Washington Block, a Victorian confection constructed in the 1880s, housed Mummery's Drug Store for many years and later the Capitol Market, as well as other familiar businesses, including Hutzel Plumbing and several photographers. Rebuilt after a fire in 1932, it was demolished in 1965 for a four-story parking structure. That structure was replaced by a new one in 1998.

WAGNER AND BIERMANN, 113 WEST WASHINGTON, C. 1895. The Wagner and Biermann machine shop west of the alley was a general repair shop for many items, including sewing machines and bicycles. It was run by men who were also gunsmiths and locksmiths. From 1917 to 1919, bicycles were sold. The building was replaced in 1920 by a brick one that houses Vogel's Locksmiths.

ANN ARBOR ORGAN WORKS

ANN ARBOR ORGAN WORKS, NORTHWEST CORNER OF FIRST AND WASHINGTON, 1872. David F. Allmendinger founded the organ works in 1872 in a shop adjoining a house purchased from Jacob Weil in 1872. By 1888 his building had expanded in several directions. Eventually, the complex was demolished, and replaced by brick factory buildings that manufactured organs, and later, pianos. The buildings still stand today taking up an entire block of First between Huron and Washington.

WEDEMEYER RADIO, 208 EAST WASHINGTON, C. 1930. In 1927, radio pioneer George Wedemeyer opened a humble radio shop in a former house and built the Wedemeyer radio there—only one example survives at the Henry Ford Museum. Wedemeyer expanded his business and today the Wedemeyer Electronics Supply Company is on South Industrial. This house has been remodeled beyond recognition and now serves as offices for Swisher Realty.

MONTGOMERY WARD BUILDING. 210–216 SOUTH FOURTH AVENUE, 1928. In 1928, workmen were putting the finishing touches on the glass in the new Montgomery Ward building on Fourth Avenue between Washington and Liberty. Ward's was a small department store, selling clothing, tires, furniture, linens, heaters, toys, and bicycles. Their specialty was a mail order department, similar to that of their rival, Sears Roebuck and Co. It was rebuilt after a terrible fire in 1950, only to be destroyed by another fire in 1960. The First National Building at Washington and Main is under construction in the background. Both buildings reflect style trends for commercial buildings in the 1920s. Light-colored terra cotta and other materials were the rage, as were decorations reminiscent of 18th-century designs, such as urns and swags. This site is now the Town Center Plaza, an arcade building with restaurants and galleries.

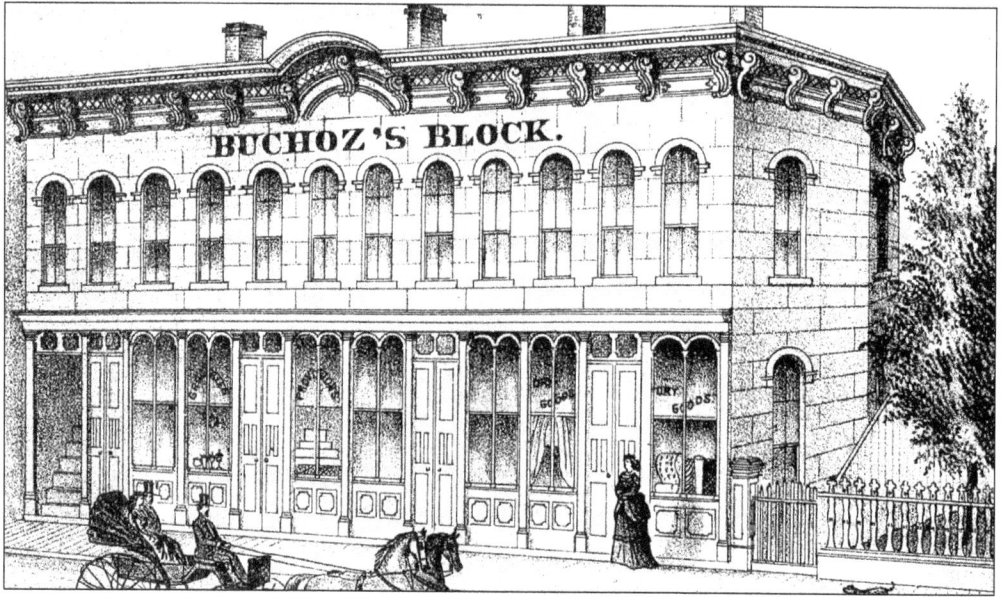

BUCHOZ'S BLOCK, DETROIT STREET AT FIFTH AVENUE, 1874. In 1851, lumber dealer Louis Buchoz erected this building, taking advantage of the increased traffic along Detroit Street following the arrival of the railroad in 1839. It was "home" to an array of German shopkeepers, such as George Ehnis, tailor; Henry Paul, cigar maker; and Stephen Reck, saloon owner. Buchoz's house was nearby and prominently featured on the 1866 Bird's-eye Map. Today the Buchoz Block site is the parking lot for Community High School.

DEMONSTRATING AN ECONOMY BALER, C. 1930. In 1911, Economy Baler, at 1254 North Main Street, began turning waste paper into profit. A "flapper" is demonstrating how it's done, using patented equipment: a paper compressor modeled on a hay baler. Started by George Langford, Economy grew to be the "largest business of its kind in the world." In 1916 they had three buildings along the river. They closed in 1976.

MAJESTIC THEATER, MAYNARD STREET, 1929. The Majestic Theater opened in 1907, one of several small theaters in the area close to campus. In addition to movies, the "Maj" had vaudeville (including the Marx Brothers and Cary Grant). This ad for the Dolph Funeral home shows the theater in its prime. The theater was demolished for the Maynard Street parking structure but Dolph's survives today as Score Keepers Bar.

FENN DRUG STORE, 103 NORTH FOREST (ZINA PITCHER NEAR WASHTENAW), 1936. This stuccoed store, built in a Spanish style with tile roof and twisted columns, once stood on what is now Zina Pitcher Street (earlier called Washtenaw Place). Clare Fenn operated the drug store from 1930 to 1965, after which it was remodeled as the Food Mart. Houses nearby hint at the residential quality of this neighborhood, obliterated long ago. Today this is the site of the U-M's Biomedical Science Research Building.

MAJESTIC THEATER INTERIOR, 1912. U-M students enjoy a show at the Majestic, a converted roller rink that could seat 1,100 and had live performances as well as silent movies. It also had dressing rooms, a confectionery, and a ladies' waiting room. Opened in 1907 with vaudeville as its main attraction, by 1913 it had switched to movies—"high class feature motion pictures"—as the manager referred to them. By 1930 they were showing "talkies," having realized that sound in movies wasn't a passing fad. In the 1920s, one of the challenges was handling the rushes of U-M students after a victorious football game. They would holler and yell and demand a free movie and usually got one. Manager Gerald Hoag, a Wolverine fan himself, hired football players as ushers and also gave the later famous Fred Waring Orchestra its first big break.

Seven

The University Expands
in All Directions

In the 20th century the university continued to expand rapidly, spreading far beyond the immediate perimeter of the original 40-acre campus. The Observatory had been built in 1854 on the edge of town, but by the first half of the 20th century the expanding campus had reached it and surrounded it. Hospital complexes grew like Topsy. (After a century of expansion, the medical system today continues to grow.) Dormitories were built. Fraternities and sororities constructed large, stylish buildings as they expanded their role on campus. Apartment buildings were constructed to house new U-M personnel. Today the expansion has reached as far as Hill on the south, parts of Washtenaw on the east, Huron on the north, and Division on the west, but these are under pressure as well. As a 1921 university publication noted ". . . and purchases go inseparably with the building program." Previous Regents had refused land offered as a gift, but "now more land must be had at once, and wisdom demands that the failure of the past. . . be replaced by statesmanlike provision for the inescapable needs of the coming decade."

Much more of the town would have been demolished had the North Campus area not been developed. In the 1950s, old farms across the Huron River were purchased with the idea of building the Residential College, a small school within the larger one, in a bucolic setting. Today, the "RC" is still close to the central campus, while North Campus is home to the Schools of Art, Music, Architecture, and Engineering, as well as several libraries.

U-M Women's Athletic Building, c. 1928. The Women's Athletic Building was built in 1928 and required the leveling of the hilly terrain that was then Palmer Field. It was part of an expanding physical education program for women after the men got a new football stadium and the IM Building. Ann Arbor architects Fry and Kasurin designed it in a Georgian style. It was demolished in 1976 and today is the site of Central Campus Recreation Building.

Women's Baseball, 1920s. Women's sports continued to expand in the 20th century and girls played baseball indoors (probably in Barbour Gym).

CATHERINE STREET HOSPITALS, GLEN AND CATHERINE LOOKING NORTHEAST, c. 1900. At the northeast corner of Glen and Catherine were the first "regular" hospital buildings built in Ann Arbor. They included a Medical Ward, the Palmer Ward and Nurses' Home, the Surgical Ward, and the Psychopathic Ward, as well as 16 other buildings. The first was erected in 1891 and the area kept growing until University Hospital on Observatory was completed in 1925. These buildings were ill-suited for their purpose and were continually criticized by medical staff, but they were a vast improvement over earlier facilities. Together with the Homeopathic Hospital, built in 1900 and now being used as North Hall by ROTC, patients had a choice of type of medical treatment. These buildings were used for many years as convalescent wards and other adjuncts to the hospital, such as the Red Cross and the School of Public Health. Today Med Sci II, the Taubman Library, and Victor Vaughan Building stand on this site.

UNIVERSITY HOSPITAL (OLD MAIN), OBSERVATORY AND ANN, C. 1925. Designed by famous Detroit architect Albert Kahn, the "new" University Hospital opened in 1925. Kahn combined a classical limestone arched entry that served as the Administration Building, with a five-armed building in the form of a double Y. Construction of the hospital required the removal of many houses of the type that can be seen in the background. The university was frugal in those days, and many of the buildings were moved. In 1986, this hospital building was demolished when the current hospital opened, just to the northeast overlooking the Huron River. Old Main's handsome stone archway, with "University Hospital" carved in its limestone lintel above the doorway, was removed for safekeeping and possible re-use. It remains in storage. Two remaining landmarks in this aerial photo are the Detroit Observatory and the Simpson Memorial Institute.

PHI RHO SIGMA, 300 NORTH INGALLS, 1917. Phi Rho Sigma, a medical fraternity, moved into the former William C. Stevens home in 1911. Stevens was vice-president of the Michigan Milling Company and Michigan State Auditor. In 1929, the 1870s building was razed and replaced with an English Tudor stone building. In 1949, that building was physically moved across the street to the southeast corner of Ingalls and Catherine to make room for an expanded St. Joseph Mercy Hospital (now the U-M's North Ingalls Building).

THETA DELTA CHI, NORTH INGALLS AT CORNWELL, C. 1920. Theta Delta Chi fraternity remodeled an older Victorian house into this Tudor Revival mansion in the early 20th century. Originally the home of Dr. Henry Simmons Frieze, it was chosen for its view of the Huron River. Featuring a clipped gable where a pointed one had been, and with half timbering replacing cut shingles, the home shared the street with St. Joseph Hospital until the hospital expanded. This sit is now a parking lot.

SIGMA PHI EPSILON, 1917. This 1917 photograph of the Sigma Phi Epsilon fraternity house is a rare view from Hill Street. The fraternity remodeled an older private home at the corner of Hill and State and remained here until the 1990s. It is now the site of the Gerald Ford School of Public Policy.

SIGMA PHI EPSILON, C. 1917. This photograph of the fraternity house is a rare view from Hill Street. The fraternity remodeled an older home at the corner of Hill and State and remained there until the 1990s. It is now the site of the U-M Gerald Ford School of Public Policy.

SIGMA PHI, 426 NORTH INGALLS, 1917. Sigma Phi, founded in 1858, is one of the oldest fraternities at the University of Michigan. In 1901 they razed an older building on the site and built a Colonial Revival style home. An article on "Ann Arbor Architecture" in the October 1901 issue of *The Inlander* noted that "the house erected by Sigma Phi fraternity is perhaps the most architecturally perfect building in Ann Arbor. . . The architect has given us an imitation of one of those beautiful colonial buildings which look down upon the Hudson, the Potomac or the James. . . The dignified grace of its columns, the flow of its lines and the simplicity of its ornaments make it a real addition to the town. . . " In 1931 it was demolished to provide parking for St. Joseph Mercy Hospital.

MY-T-FINE CAFÉ, 101 SOUTH THAYER STREET, 1921. Until 1956, Thayer Street was continuous between Washington and Huron, filled with houses and small businesses such as the My-T-Fine Café behind the then-Ann Arbor High School. The university built an addition to the former high school, renamed the Frieze Building, and the street was eliminated. The My-T-Fine had vanished long before.

MY-T-FINE CAFÉ INTERIOR, 1921. Known also as Mrs. De Barr's café, little cafes like this one dotted the town and served standard American food. When the owners retired, they sold to Glen Davenport, originator of the White Spot on East William, which eventually became Red's Rite Spot, a legendary campus eatery. Alas, it too had to go, for the construction of Tower Plaza at Maynard and William in 1968.

108

Eight

Washtenaw Avenue Remains an Elite Street

Throughout the 19th and part of the 20th century, Washtenaw Avenue was a dirt road going to Ypsilanti, lined with farms and private homes. In fact, it was once called the Ypsilanti Road. By the mid-19th century, prosperous dairy and fruit farmers erected substantial homes set amongst beautiful gardens with groves of trees. This road also appealed to the more romantic University professors who preferred living in the country. In the late 19th century, fraternities and sororities began to occupy some of these mansions—and later demolished them to build more modern buildings.

The Washtenaw-Hill Historic District protects some surviving buildings, but others have been lost. Despite their disappearance, the street has managed to maintain its residential character. It is still a lovely, tree-lined street, a gracious entry to our town.

ISRAEL AND OLIVIA HALL HOUSE, 1129 WASHTENAW, 1880S. Real estate broker Israel Hall built this late Italianate house c. 1874 and resided here until his death in 1890. His widow Olivia continued to live here until her death in 1908. Originally from Toledo, Hall became one of Ann Arbor's most prominent citizens, and a particular supporter of the school system. One biography noted that "his labors were effective in furthering the cause of public education," but that "many other lines, however, felt the stimulus of his energy. . . " In 1917 the house became the Phi Chi fraternity and it was also used as the Ann Arbor Private Hospital run by Mrs. Margaret Kelly. The house was demolished for construction of the U-M Ruthven Museums Building which opened in 1928.

OLIVIA AND ISRAEL HALL, 1129 WASHTENAW, 1880s. The Halls posed for this portrait shortly before Israel died, surrounded by eclectic objects typical of a Victorian interior. Mrs. Hall was active in many organizations, particularly women'ssuffrage groups. She was a gracious hostess and on four occasions between 1877 and 1890 gave receptions for Women's Rights advocate Susan B. Anthony. She even sold land in Arkansas to finance the cause. Olivia also developed part of the Burns Park neighborhood. She and her husband purchased the house at 1530 Hill Street in 1876, along with the lands of the J.D. Baldwin fruit farm. Son Louis was given the house as a wedding gift in 1885. In the 1890s she purchased the old fairgrounds, platted it as Olivia B. Hall's subdivisions #1 and #2. She sold many lots with 60-foot setback requirements which today lend grace and character to the area. She also built and sold many residences. Olivia Street perpetuates her name. Cambridge Street was originally named Israel Avenue in honor of her husband.

HALL INTERIOR, 1129 WASHTENAW, 1880s. A view of the interior of the Israel and Olivia Hall home shows a variety of furniture and objects, typical of homes of the wealthy in the 1880s and 1890s. Portraits of family members, Grecian urns, glass-globed gas chandeliers, heavy drapery, statuary, and ornate furniture are all characteristic of the late Victorian era.

HALL GRANDCHILDREN WITH TOYS, 1880s. These children, probably the Halls' grandchildren, are playing with their hobbyhorses and other toys in this charming picture. The ornate and busy interior may seem a potential disaster area for small children but they seem to make it work. Son Louis P. Hall became a Professor of Dentistry, active in various dental associations.

JUDGE WILLIAM D. HARRIMAN HOUSE, 1219 WASHTENAW, 1933. Judge Harriman, a native of Vermont, built this grand Second Empire home in 1870, shortly after moving from California. He was elected mayor of Ann Arbor three times and also Probate Judge. The University purchased the house in 1926 to be a residence for women and the name was changed to Mary Markley House. In 1950 it was closed and a new dorm was built elsewhere with the same name. Today it is an island of trees and flowers bounded by Washtenaw Court and Geddes.

ALUMNAE HOUSE, 1233 WASHTENAW, 1918. The university purchased this Italianate mansion in 1917 to provide housing for women. After U-M purchased the Harriman House in 1926, the women moved there and this house was demolished. It was built in 1868 by Charles T. Wilmot, a Connecticut native and farmer turned developer whose name is perpetuated in nearby Wilmot Street.

113

ANDREW TEN BROOK HOUSE, 1437 WASHTENAW (AT SOUTH UNIVERSITY), 1874. An engraving from the 1874 *Washtenaw County Atlas* gives an idealistic rendering of the leafy setting of Professor Ten Brook's 1860s home. A native of Elmira, New York, and of Dutch ancestry, Ten Brook arrived in Ann Arbor in 1844, already ordained a pastor in Detroit's First Baptist Church. His hiring was controversial among the Methodists on the board of Regents. His arrival coincided with enrollment of the University's first senior class—a total of eleven. In the 1850s he went to Europe where he served as U.S. consul in Munich, returning to head the U-M library in 1864 on his 50th birthday. Ten Brook had a keen interest in local history, and for 50 years collected and published materials about Washtenaw County and Ann Arbor. He died in 1899. This home was demolished and replaced in 1904 by a Colonial Revival fraternity house built by Phi Delta Theta.

ISAAC NEWTON DEMMON RESIDENCE, 1432 WASHTENAW, 1917. Demmon, a professor at the University of Michigan for 45 years, leans against a tree in front of the house he bought in 1880. It was built in the 1850s by Professor James R. Boise, a Greek scholar dedicated to plain living. Demmon greatly improved the property and it was described as one of the most picturesque, pleasant, and cultivated of Ann Arbor's homes. Demmon came to Ann Arbor in 1872 as an instructor in mathematics, and also served as principal of the Ann Arbor High School. Later he was a professor of history, becoming head of the English Department in 1881. He hosted poet Robert Frost in 1921, during one of his residencies in Ann Arbor. This home was demolished and replaced in 1937 by the First Presbyterian Church. Demmon's memorial in the 1921 *Michigan Alumnus* ran nine pages. His colleagues noted his death "crowned a life of incessant labor, and enriched by such a depth of experience as few men, and only big men, can know."

CHAUNCEY MILLEN HOUSE, 1550 WASHTENAW, 1864. Chauncey Millen, U.S. Collector of Internal Revenue and a dealer in dry goods and groceries, built this Gothic Revival/Italianate mansion in 1861. It was new when this engraving appeared in the 1864 *Washtenaw County Plat Map*. Purportedly, it was designed by famous Philadelphia architect Samuel Sloan, who had a national reputation— it did appear in his book, *The Model Architect*, 1861. Millen was a former sea captain who came to Ann Arbor in the 1860s and opened a clothing store on Main Street. His son Charles continued in business in the 1880s with D. Fred Schairer as Schairer and Millen. In the 1890s the home was sold to the Phi Kappa Psi Fraternity.

116

MILLEN HOME AS PHI KAPPA PSI, 1917. The men of Phi Kappa Psi can be seen standing on the entry gates to the former Millen estate. Founded at Jefferson College, the Alpha Chapter was established at the University of Michigan in 1876. The fraternity purchased the property in 1892 and in an 1896 booklet, residents were described as living in "a large, roomy building at the corner of Hill street [sic] and Washtenaw Ave." The building was torn down in 1919 and replaced with a Tudor Revival house that still stands today.

BROWN-LLOYD HOUSE, 1735 WASHTENAW (CORNER OF CAMBRIDGE), 1939. Associated for many years with U-M Dean and Acting President Alfred H. Lloyd, and his daughter Alice Crocker Lloyd, Dean of Women, this house was built by Hiram Brown in 1851 in the Greek Revival style. As a stucco-over-brick building, it resembled those built on the original U-M campus. The house had belonged earlier to the Benjamin Day family and was purchased in 1901 by the Lloyds. "Beautifully kept up, with spacious grounds and fine old trees, this pioneer house still performs its daily function which only age and tradition can give," wrote the *Michigan Alumnus* in February 1933. Miss Lloyd died in 1950, and in 1960 the house was razed for a new chapter house of the Alpha Chi Omega sorority. A newspaper account of the impending demolition noted that many in town were buying pieces of the house, such as stained glass windows, doors, and fixtures. It was drawn and measured for the Historic American Buildings Survey (HABS) in 1933 under the direction of Professor Emil Lorch.

EVART SCOTT HOUSE, 1830 WASHTENAW, 1890s. Evart Scott built this farmhouse around 1876, on what was still township land. Scott came to Ann Arbor in 1868 from Ohio and became a successful businessman, civic activist, and farmer. He planted many elms along Washtenaw shortly after establishing his Elm Fruit Farm on 30 acres at the city limits. In 1915, when the area was annexed into the city, Scott sold most of the acreage to developer Charles Spooner. With the assistance of architect Fiske Kimball, Spooner created the Ives Woods subdivision, which still has many of the elegant homes built then. Scott's house was sold around 1925 to Dr. R. Bishop Canfield, a professor in the U-M Medical School, who updated it to a Colonial Revival style with the help of Lewis J. Boynton, a professor in the Architecture School. In 1951, the house was acquired by the Ann Arbor Women's City Club, which hired local architect Ralph Hammett to design an addition in 1958. Somewhere under the current exterior lie the bones of Evart Scott's old home.

D'Ooge House, 1523 Washtenaw, 1890s. Professors Martin L. and Benjamin L. D'Ooge erected this home around 1870 on a very large lot. Martin Luther D'Ooge (a Dutch name) joined the U-M faculty in 1867 and remained in charge of the Department of Greek for almost 45 years. Benjamin taught briefly at the U-M and then at Ypsilanti. It was a charming country house, complete with covered porch and decorative bargeboard on the front gable. It was also one of the houses that hosted Robert Frost when he was Poet-in-Residence at the university in the early 1920s. Martin died in 1915 and Mrs. D'Ooge resided here in her widowhood for another 30 years until her death c. 1948. The house was demolished shortly thereafter and replaced by the University Lutheran Chapel in 1949. Around 1954, the Chi Omega sorority built their new home on land from this site.

Nine

Gone but Not Forgotten

While demolitions of several Ann Arbor buildings provoked controversy and sadness, several were catalysts for political actions. Destruction of the Henry Carter Adams house in 1986, by the First Presbyterian Church, actually started the political career of State Senator Liz Brater. Other demolitions, such as that of the Barbour-Waterman Gymnasiums in 1976, created incentives for listing on the National Register of Historic Places. Loss of the Bertha Muehlig house on Main Street in 1962 prompted the creation of the Ann Arbor Historical Commission, which became the Historic District Commission in 1971, shortly after the demolition of the Goodrich House on State Street in that year. Sadly, the University of Michigan is not required to abide by local historic district designation, and this continues to be a cause of worry when the U-M acquires landmark buildings. On the whole, the University has been respectful of its historic landmarks, and has recently restored gems like the Observatory, Hill Auditorium, Rackham Auditorium, the Burnham House, Lane Hall, and the Kelsey Museum for the future generations to enjoy. Ann Arbor's older buildings are part of the fabric of Ann Arbor's history and deserve to be protected and respected.

MUEHLIG HOUSES, 311 AND 315 SOUTH MAIN STREET, C. 1910. Florian Muehlig arrived from Swabia in 1840 and in 1852 started a furniture and coffin business with his brother, John, which became the Muehlig Funeral Home of today. Florian built the small house at 311 South Main in 1840 and lived there with many of his children. In 1872, he purchased 315 South Main which was probably built in the 1840s. His granddaughter, Bertha E. Muehlig, resided at 315 until her death in 1955. The house was Greek Revival, in the stucco-over-brick style so popular in Ann Arbor. According to Architecture Professor Emil Lorch, "the simple dignity of the house resembled that of several former Ann Arbor houses. It is the sole remaining house of what was long a residential section." Lorch praised its proportions and simple gable returns, and had it drawn in the 1930s for the Historic American Buildings Survey.

BERTHA E. MUEHLIG HOUSE, 315 SOUTH MAIN STREET, C. 1910. Miss Muehlig was a beloved philanthropist who ran a successful dry goods business at 126 South Main Street which she bought in 1911 and renamed B.E. Muehlig, Inc. She was "Santa Claus" to all and voted "Ann Arbor's Greatest Woman." An avid supporter of public education, she often treated children to Christmas parties. Her store remained in business until the 1980s, long after her death in 1955. Demolition of her house in 1962 by the Glidden Paint Company for a new store upset many and sparked a new interest in historic preservation which eventually led to the creation of the Historic District Commission. Ann Arbor historian Lela Duff wrote in her book *Ann Arbor Yesterdays* (1962): "The whole town grieved, not only at the passing of a beautiful and historic landmark, but at the loss of a visible reminder of the noble and gracious woman who had lived there." A one-story commercial building occupies the site today.

HENRY CARTER ADAMS HOUSE, 1421 HILL STREET, 1920S. U-M Economics Professor Henry Carter Adams, a giant in his field, wrote his mother in 1894 that he was erecting "a colonial building of the purest type. The roof has no turret, tower nor any other disfigurement. . . no curves, no spindle work or geegaws." Adams joined several colleagues who were building houses without "geegaws" on the newly subdivided Hill Street. Born in Iowa, Adams got his degree at Johns Hopkins, and came to Ann Arbor in 1886. He built a distinguished economics department that achieved a national reputation. He was chief statistician to the Interstate Commerce Commission and as such implemented a system governing railway accounts that led to other levels of public regulation. Adams was also a co-founder of the American Economic Association. It was his goal to bring the best elements of European thought to bear on current problems in the U.S. He died in 1921 and his widow continued to live in the house until her death in 1962. The First Presbyterian Church soon owned the property and encouraged the creation of a coffeehouse with music, now the nationally-known Ark Coffeehouse located on Main Street. The church's demolition of the house in 1986 generated much controversy and bitterness. Today this block is part of the Washtenaw-Hill Historic District.

INTERIOR, HENRY CARTER ADAMS HOUSE, 1421 HILL, C. 1920. Adams helped design the first railway system in China. The simple interior matched the exterior and the Chinese screen and table blended with the other simple furnishings. First Presbyterian Church bought the property in 1969, and until 1984 it was home of the Ark Coffeehouse, which offered folk music performances. In 1986 the church razed the house and the lot remains empty today.

RAZING OF THE HENRY CARTER ADAMS HOUSE, APRIL 28, 1986. Despite public outcry, leaders of the Presbyterian Church proceeded with demolition plans. As one publication noted, "Citizens across Ann Arbor were saddened at the action of First Presbyterian Church. . . (The Adams house) was widely prized as a key structure. . . What made the church's action particularly outrageous to many was that it had no pressing need for land."

AMARIAH FREEMAN HOUSE, 1315 HILL STREET, 1915. In 1908, attorney Amariah Freeman built this house and lived in it with wife Clara for only six years. He then built a larger house on the southeast corner of Hill and East University and sold this one to the Alpha Sigma Phi fraternity. The photo shows the house shortly after the fraternity purchased it. Designed in an Italian Renaissance style, it had characteristic features of the style including a triple arcade, large arched windows, red brick quoins, stucco walls, and red clay tiles on a hipped roof. It had an interesting floor plan, designed like an Italian palazzo around an open courtyard. Large houses like this, on deep, wooded lots were common on Hill Street. The fraternity used it until 1941. It later was a rooming house and then sold in 1986 to Delta Sigma Phi Fraternity. The fraternity abandoned it in 1994 when they couldn't afford repairs to meet City Code. It became a hangout for the homeless and a fire set by vagrants in 1994 heavily damaged the building. It was demolished in 1999. The site is still empty.

126

THE PLANADA APARTMENTS, 1127 EAST ANN STREET, 2003. By 1929, apartment living had reached its peak before the Depression put a stop to most construction. The last of its kind, the Planada was typical of many apartment structures built in the 1920s. Spanish Revival-style with clay tiles on the roof, casement windows, and a shaped pediment, it was first home to medical professionals. Later it served many types of residents in its 28 apartments. The University demolished it in 2003 for parking.

DETAIL OF THE PLANADA APARTMENTS, 1127 EAST ANN STREET, 2003. A typical feature of the Spanish Revival style is wrought iron, which can be seen on one of the balconies. Every row of windows was of a different shape and style, sporting Romanesque details. Although designated a historic structure by the city, purchase by the University spelled its doom. The site will hold a parking structure.

PHOTO CREDITS

All references, unless otherwise noted, are to collections in the Bentley Historical Library of the University of Michigan.

Pages two and four: UCCs and *Washtenaw County Michigan Plat Maps 1856 and 1864*.

Chapter One: George Swain, *Washtenaw County Michigan Plat Maps 1856 and 1864*, Sam Sturgis, *Ann Arbor News*, Advertising Cards, Post Card Collection. Other: Robert Samborski.

Chapter Two: Mel Ivory, Sturgis, Vertical File, Michigan Alumni Association, U-M Photos Vertical File, *The Castilian*, Washtenaw Historical Society, Swain.

Chapter Three: Ann Arbor Photograph Vertical File, Swain, Ivory, Sturgis, *Michigan Alumnus*, *Michiganensian*, *1893 Art Work of Washtenaw County*, State Savings Bank Booklet, William Lewis Collection, *Washtenaw County Michigan Plat Maps 1856 and 1864*, *1874 Combined Atlas of Washtenaw County*.

Chapter Four: Photographic Vertical File, *1874 Combined Atlas of Washtenaw County*, Emil Lorch, Ivory, Lucy Chapin Collection, Sturgis, U-M Alumni Association, Post Card Collection. Other: Robert Samborski.

Chapter Five: *1893 Artwork of Washtenaw County*, Sturgis, Advertising Cards, Buss, Ivory, *Ann Arbor News*, Washtenaw Historical Society, *Washtenaw County Michigan Plat Maps 1856 and 1864*, Swain, Lorch. Other: Oscar Buss, Carol Horn (William and Edna Horn Archive), Wystan Stevens, Robert Samborski, Ralph Beebe.

Chapter Six: Swain, *Michigan History Magazine*, S.D. Townley Photo Album, 1874 Combined Atlas of Washtenaw County, Sturgis, Vertical File, U-M Women's Athletic Association, Washtenaw Historical Society, Ivory, Post Card Collection. Other: *Ann Arbor: The First Hundred Years* (O.W. Stephenson, 1927), History of the Congregational Church, Robert Samborski.

Chapter Seven: U-M Women's Athletic Association, Swain. Other: Ann Arbor District Library.

Chapter Eight: Sturgis, Swain, *1874 Combined Atlas of Washtenaw County*, *Washtenaw County Michigan Plat Maps 1856 and 1864*, *Michiganensian*, Howell Taylor Collection, Post Card Collection, *Michigan Alumnus*.

Chapter Nine: Washtenaw Historical Society, Sturgis, Henry Carter Adams Collection, Swain. Other: Lisa Dengiz, Rob Goodspeed (Goodspeed Update).

www.ingramcontent.com/pod-product-compliance
Lightning Source LLC
Chambersburg PA
CBHW050650110426

42813CB00007B/1968